I0827401

8T
How On Earth Do We Speak?

Praise for Mary E. Carter's Books

"... by turns very funny and very serious, confident and uncompromisingly weird, Mary E. Carter has a voice with unquestionable power and we look forward to reading more from her."

— *Jewish Book Council*

"Carter's *Diaspora of the Discombobulated* 2024 is lively, thought-provoking, and spiked with humorous wordplay."

— David Steinberg, *Albuquerque Journal*

"... *I, Sarah Steinway* 2018 a page-turning portrait of a woman surviving the apocalypse, is hauntingly memorable."

— *Publisher's Weekly*

"Mary E. Carter's characters in her novel, *The Three-Day Departure of Mrs. Annette Zinn* 2019 have a *pintele yid*: a spark of Jewishness that helps them navigate this complex world with sensitivity."

— *Rabbi Jack Shlachter, New Mexico*

"Accolades for writing the most charming book on copyright certainly go to Mary E. Carter, a graphic designer who should also receive a bravery award for tackling the subject of copyright without a law degree . . . Carter navigates the legal issues with dexterity in her *Electronic Highway Robbery* by Peachpit Press 1996."

— Tad Crawford, *Communication Arts Magazine*

Also by Mary E. Carter

Electronic Highway Robbery

A Non-Swimmer Considers Her Mikvah

I, Sarah Steinway

All Good Tova Goodman Revised Edition

The Three-Day Departure of Mrs. Annette Zinn

Diaspora of the Discombobulated

A Death Delayed

A Non-Swimmer Plunges Deeper Into Her Mikvah

Midrash, Memory, Commentary?

Mary E. Carter

ISBN: 979-8-234-04059-6

Printed in the USA

The following sources for excerpts are used with permission of Mary E. Carter:

A Death Delayed — Agent Orange: Hidden Killer of Vietnam
Copyright © 2017 Mary E. Carer
ISBN-13: 978-0692913840

A Non-Swimmer Considers Her Mikvah
Copyright © 2024 Mary E. Carter
ISBN 978-0-692-26582-6

A Non-Swimmer Plunges Deeper Into Her Mikvah
Surviving the Unfathomable Depths of October 7, 2023
Copyright © 2024 Mary E. Carter
ISBN 979-8-218-47316-7

Molting
Posted by Chicken Lady on The WELL, 1995
From Mary E. Carter's essays and blog on The WELL as The Chicken Lady

The Three-Day Departure of Mrs. Annette Zinn
Copyright © 2019 Mary E. Carter
ISBN 9780578521930

Diaspora of the Discombobulated
Copyright © 2024 Mary E. Carter
ISBN 9798218233129

I, Sarah Steinway
Copyright © 2018 Mary E. Carter
ISBN 978-0-692-98524-3

All Good Tova Goodman Revised Edition
Copyright 2022 Mary E. Carter
ISBN 9780578376875

To Joann O.

How on Earth did we talk,

to tell, over time,

what was bound in time?

My mother died . . . and that fact has shaped my life.
All that I have become and much that I have not become,
I trace directly or indirectly to her death.

— Dr. Sherwin B. Nuland, *How We Die*

It was charm again, my dear,
simple, creamy English charm . . .
Charm is the great English blight . . .
It spots and kills anything it touches.
It kills love: it kills art . . .
I greatly fear . . . it has killed you.

— Evelyn Waugh, *Brideshead Revisited*

I am older than I once was, younger than I will be.
That's not unusual nor is it strange,
That after changes upon changes,
We are more or less the same.

Lyrics from Simon and Garfunkel's *The Boxer*

Even in our sleep, pain which cannot forget
falls drop by drop upon the heart,
until, in our own despair,
against our will,
comes wisdom
through the awful grace of God.

— Robert F. Kennedy quoting Aeschylus
after 1968 assassination of Martin Luther King, Jr.

Sunrise has no voice.

Sunset neither.

Yet they may speak of something,

Voiceless.

Given time.

Sunrise Sunset

Sunrise

Sunset

As ever.

Sunshine.

Moonshine.

Both may tell, one day,

What was bound in Silence.

In Silence Bound

Alright. Alright. All right. Already. All ready.

I will speak now with my own voice in this book.

No more with the dinner party question that goes like this:

"Ah so. You write novels. Do you write about yourself in all your books?"

As if. As if to disparage, in a sly way, my creativity, or whatever, in the task of telling story. 'Just asking.'

As if and of course: Men write about things LARGE. Women write tearoom dramas, *small stuff.*

As if creating fiction, in which I, the woman author, embed myself within the narrative arc, were a mere breeze. Easy-peasy.

As if.

Yet, here's a thought, on second thought: what if I include in this memoir excerpts from each of my fiction books that may demonstrate that I do, indeed and at times, use material from my own life to create my fictions? That's an idea. Let's see if it works. Stay tuned.

So I have gathered together all the strands I can manage in

my meagre hands and this, now, is a bunch of those stories, all run together. Maybe not in order. Not orderly. But they are my stories. Under my name as author of this volume. These stories are mine. My words. My memories. My take on my eighty years. Texting? 8T.

Cranky? You think I sound cranky? Well, I'm entitled. A lot of stuff has gone down for lo my eighty years. It's a load to carry. Plaudits, too, for celebration. But, hey, I'm game. I'm going to give it a GO. So, stick around for dessert. If I can dredge one up.

First of all I have earned Bragging Rights. I'm gonna be eighty. I have earned all my plaudits, as well as my fair share of sniggers and snorts, all of it for who I am. For who I have been. I may be regarded by some as a pissant. Or moderately noteworthy, bit of a smalltime winner. Sunrise and sunset and ten year's of fog, forsaken in fugue. Career bumps, mostly up. Finally, the big bucks.

Sunshine.Moonshine. Both may tell, one day, what has been bound in Silence.

Sunshine. Moonshine. Both may tell, one day, what has been bound in Silence. A significant birthday. Time to ruminate. Chuckle ruefully. Shrug. Rummage. Boil. Rinse. Repeat.

As a way to stay in touch with my friends, every morning I post a picture in a text, sent separately to each one on my list.

No comments are required. Most of my pictures are those I take with my little cellphone. I keep it in my back jeans pocket or my loose floppy pajama side pocket and I slide it out most mornings or evenings to capture sunrise, sunset. Just a reminder that it has been, or will be, another day and here we all are, still, and it is, indeed, another day.

Either or any which way, well, let's just take a look. No equivocation. Few surprises. But well and true, here's my life at eighty. Not the whole biography. But bits and pieces. Chunks and wallops. Odds and ends. Memorial bits. But, hey: who'd a-thunk? I'm heading for my eighties. Wow! Sigh.

1967
First Question

A ragtag group of us are dragging-ass along an overtrodden pathway toward a bedraggled football field. On that day the bleachers around that field are cheek-by-jowl with hundreds of graduation fans, the long-suffering parents of those longtime college students. Finally. It's graduation day. We, the rag-tag milieu trudging along here, are adorned in tasseled rental headgear, standard for these ceremonies, headed in our headgear into our singular unknowns, each and every one of us, individuals, but at this moment, at this point in the ceremonies, simply a single dispirited gathering, now deemed as successful graduates, heading, head-geared, finally, from our higher educations. Great. Just great.

"Thank God!"

The fans and supporters of these latest graduates breathe a sigh of relief. At last. And we still have bank accounts, leaner of course, but still in tact. We're done! Sighs of relief.

Graduates. But to what? The word graduate – the verb – contains the sense of being propelled forward.

A commencement. Yes. That's the word they will use today. Commencement is the battered word that our elders will use to honor our achievements during this ceremony. Nice collegiate-sounding word. College education – something you can always fall back on.

Hey, you know what? During each of the several job interviews I attended in years to come, not a single interviewer ever asked me about my college education. Not ONE. Not EVER. And there it sat, nicely displayed, on the bottom of the page of my evolving professional resumes. Mary E. Carter, Bachelor of Arts, 1967.

Commencement. Into what? Yet here's the thing: since that day in June 1967, never once have I forgotten the words said to me by a young man I had known only as one of the roommates of the last of my erstwhile very-great-loves during my senior year.

In front of me, in alphabetical order, strode Marc, commencing into what, we did not know. Marc was a very large man with a black beard and longish dark hair. He had snoozed throughout several semesters of Art History. Never said a word to me that senior year. I was too busy paying rapt attention to Marc's roommate, another example of my dubious judgment of that era. I never said anything at all to roommate Marc. Nor he to me. I could foresee nothing about my commencement. It's easy, but dispiriting to me, to reflect back on that year and to retrospectively conclude that, pretty soon, my commencement was to be my ultimate year of separation from every single idea, concept, preconceived notion, of my entire education and of my previous life, not to mention to the whole of my family life up to that point. My mother and father were seated out there in the bleachers, watching us come down that path to our commencements. My graduation was to be the last celebratory event that we would have as a family. All of it was soon to die. I could never have predicted, during that long walk, how my life, my very persona, would take such a drastic turn. The walk toward my graduation ceremony would turn out to be, in effect, a funeral procession for my family life up to that moment. I could never, at that graduation event, have even for a moment conceived of such a sad ceremony of passage.

Marc, clutching his small black leather case that contained his actual graduation certificate, turned to me and said:

"What are we going to do now, Mary Carter?"

And of course, of course, I have never forgotten his question. Marc's timing would turn out to be portentous. Yet, in retrospect, here in my eighth decade, I realize that his words were influenced by the symbols of that environment, the long walk down a well-trodden path, our regalia, robes we had never worn before, red tassels dangling like spiders from ill-fitting rectangles. The entire ill-fated, wholly inappropriate, yet highly traditional, commencement ceremony, included formal speeches:

" . . . go out there you students and live your happy and accomplished lives, always remember . . ."

A veritable blast of trite similes and clichés were hurtled at us by those who were, supposedly, our well-educated superiors. I have often thought of Marc's words. And lately, I have thought more and more about them, especially since they stood out after having to listen to all that bilgewater.

"What are we going to do now, Mary Carter?"

How on Earth did Marc speak so plainly? What made him ask this question? Were those to be his last words? It turned out that they were, in real life, very nearly, his last words. Then he died. Not even a few weeks after our procession. Likely of his own intention. He crashed in his own airplane. Likely a Cessna. He, nor I, would ever be again the two people we had momentarily been during college. And certainly, during that procession toward our diplomas, into future lives, decorated with red tassels on peculiar square headgear — we would never again be who we had been on that day.

"What are we going to do now, Mary Carter?"

That question. I shiver remembering, repeating it for decades. How inconceivable to me, in the moment that Marc spoke to me and asked his question, how utterly impossible for me, trodding down that well-worn path to our commencement, how inconceivable back then, despite my so-called education, art major, psych minor, for me to have understood the sorrowful predilection of Marc's or my futures. How on Earth did Marc know what to say? Why on Earth did Marc ask me that huge question? Despite my stupidity, chuckleheaded graduate of higher education that I had become, I simply have forever remembered his last words, his question. How come? Why? Little did we, either of us, know what we were about to commence upon.

Sunrise. Sunset. Sunrise. Sunset.

What *was* I going to do now?

But then this: now in my 80th season of springtime dawning I see yet something new in Marc's question to me. He alone of all the men I had known up to that point, Marc alone was a man who asked me something fundamental about my life. Marc alone asked me a question about me. No other man — were they really men? — had ever asked me such a probing question. And I hadn't even noticed. Until now.

What a marvelous question.

Ah-Ha!

The very idea of a man ever asking me a meaningful question about my most fundamentally held 'notions' had not even been among my former lovers. And so I spent a lifetime railing about how little my former lovers really cared about the most formative elements of my very being as a human being. Floundering I had always been. 'Til now. And Marc had not been even a former loved one of mine. Foolish girl. Foolish graduate from higher, so-called, education. What a dunderhead.

Even our friend Nina made this point about her former lovers:

"I never had a single conversation about any single thing that was important to my soul with men back then."

They never asked the right questions:

"What are we going to do now, Mary Carter?"

Realizing I am a subscriber to ancestry.com, I clicked over there and found a scant few items that are records of Marc. Here is the most explanatory, published in a local newspaper a couple of days after Marc died in 1967. "*. . .killed in an airplane crash . . . in California."*

I grew into my potential late in my life. At least I can say this: At Last.

"What are we going to do now, Mary Carter?"

Odd that I kept his words in mind all these decades. The dates of his life and death on ancestry.com were definitely his, as was his complete name. How on Earth did he speak? Why on Earth have I remembered? And why now? What a peculiar search to initiate here and now that I am in my eighth decade.

What are we going to do now, Mary Carter?:

Before moving in with Gary in 1974.We marry two years later.

What are we going to do now, Mary Carter?:

Before celebrating our 50th anniversary.

What are we going to do now, Mary Carter?:

Before life-saving surgery.

What are we going to do now, Mary Carter?:

Before leaving my career as an advertising copywriter to paint and write.

What are we going to do now, Mary Carter?:

After my mother's funeral.

What are we going to do now, Mary Carter?:

Now that you're turning 80.

Functionally illiterate, leaning slovenly, not quite conscious, moving as if in a trance, pressing toward comfy philistinism, off I marched towards life. Either education had failed me or I it.

I shuffled up to the stage, gathered my graduation certificate, trod offstage and just a few feet in front of me Marc turned, looking over his right shoulder, twisting back toward me, still stepping forward, and he asked me:

"What are we going to do now, Mary Carter?"

That was the one thing said on that singular significant day that stuck. It's stuck with me, now in my eightieth year, still. But very sadly so, I hadn't understood it at the time. It's all I can do to understand those words, Marc's words, right now.

Tradition, or is it journalism, or is it grammar, or is it

professors of Lit — well it is something persistent and it goes like this: we who write must categorize and label our words as Fiction — novels and fairy tales, poems perhaps? Or Non-Fiction — autobiographies, memoirs, histories, science, statistics. Serious stuff vs. once-upon-a-timey stuff.

But what about this wobbly ground, that of those of us who became defined by and based on what we were fed. Labeling became de riguer. Your teachers asked:

"Is this real? Or did you make this up?"

And by fed, additionally, I extend my meaning of the word fed to the entire fifties thing. Born after a big war, we digested a steady diet of yummy fifties overweening, over-confidence. Oh yes, we were the winners of that world war. We conquered. We won. We knew it all. And that's a fact. Ah, the hubris. The strutting, the cock-surety of every damned and blessed thing or idea or concept. And it was all laid upon us kids as we stared mindless, slack-jawed, into this new picture tube world, brand new devices delivering the aforementioned messages to our gullible little selves. Manipulated we were. And we didn't even notice.

So, what then about a life, mine for example, what then was Fiction? What was Non? Was it Fiction — our swing sets, our gentle walk four blocks past picturesque identical cheaply crafted little doll houses, off to school, our Sears catalog of plaid dresses. Or was it Non? Worlds over there, spin that globe, and it is unimaginable to a girl, nine years old, whose world was so cosseted, all wrapped up in the gentle pink bunting of the overconfidence of that time.

"You can do anything you put your mind to." So my mother told me back then.

With my lifetime encumbered by all of this cultural detritus, I grew into my potential late in life. At least I can say this: At Last.

After my mikvah I heard Marc's question again:

"What are we going to do now, Mary Carter?"

After my latest novel:

"What are we going to do now, Mary Carter?"

I am Not a Rabbi, BUT

This sliver of midrash, my own take on the familiar *Torah* portion referred to as the Binding of Isaac, or the Akedah, will provide a portal as we set off to discover the roots of how on Earth we speak. The hinge goes either way through this portal: agree or disagree. Take your pick. But listen, if you will, to my take on how on Earth we speak.

I am not a rabbi BUT. I am ever a student of *Torah*. I have pledged to read with attention and intention so that I may eventually understand, more fully, the meaning of these sacred words and their narratives. Over time I discover more and more meaning during my annual readings. This year during these High Holy Days I have new observations and possible questions and I have come to new conclusions about the *Akedah, Genesis 22* and *23*. Did you know that before she was called Sarah her name was Sarai? Well, it's true. I like that. She and I both changed names when we bound ourselves to our Jewish heritage. So the *Akedah* is aimed directly at me. More or less. Right? Well, so I like to think. This takes me right back to the question: Did Sarah set an example to mothers

NOT to tell all? Or is it something else? I ask questions. I am not called The Maven of Midrash for naught! Admittedly, I agree that there have been times when my fellow students of *Torah*, have called me by that title and not without a bit of good-natured mockery.

Long ago I sat at a large mahogany table in a Rabbi's study and all six of us, all women that day, shouted out at this last line in *Torah* featuring Sarah. I mean we yelled and we shouted in disbelief at the words of Sarah in *Chapter 23:1*

"And Sarah's life was a hundred and twenty-seven years, the years of Sarah's life."

BUT WHAT-THE-HECK-DID-SARAH-SAY???

That's It?

That's All?

Sarah says *nothing* to her ever-loving husband after — it may be assumed — he tells her what they had been doing. What he, her husband, had been prepared to DO to their son, Isaac — Sarah's son of her very advanced years? And not a peep? Not a dish thrown from her hand in the direction of Abraham's head. Nothing? Not a word? Not a full-blown spat, or should I say 'altercation' — if there had been one, between husband and wife? What woman on Earth, or down through the generations of Jewish women who study *Torah,* even today, would not have responded to such a spousal confession?

"That's it?"

Not a word from Sarah after the event, presumably, when she hears about this horrifying near-miss involved in the potential killing/sacrificing of Isaac, her beloved son of her elder years? The narrative of the *Akedah* is told from the point of view of Abraham and, in his supporting role, as a sacrificial victim, of Isaac. He wonders aloud to his father about the absence of a sheep for the offering.

Here is the quote from the narrative-of-record, found in *Torah* for the story of the Binding of Isaac, the Akedah, and it reads thus:

> "GENESIS CHAPTER 22: *And it happened after these things that God tested Abraham. And He said to him, "Abraham!" and he said, "Here I am." And He said, "Take, pray, your son, your only one, whom you love, Isaac, and go forth to the land of Moriah and offer him up as a burnt offering on one of the mountains which I shall say to you." And Abraham rose early in the morning and saddled his donkey and took his two lads with him, and Isaac his son, and the split wood for the offering, and rose and went to the place that God had said to him. . . . Abraham took the wood for the offering and put it on Isaac his son and he took in his hand the fire and the cleaver, and the two of them went together. And Isaac said to Abraham his father, "Father! And he said,*
>
> *"Here I am, my son."*

> *And he said "here is the fire and the wood but where is the sheep for the offering?"*
>
> *And Abraham said, "God will see to the sheep for the offering, my son."*

In summary: Abraham takes Isaac off to off him. Right? Obedient to God's request. And off they go. Yet, only by the will of God, or the lack of decisiveness thereof, or the interjection of an angel – do we believe in angels – the sacrifice of Isaac, so-called, was halted. It varies, depending upon your translation, the words in *Torah* may read:

". . . but out of the heaven an angel of G-d called to him,. . ."

Or:

"And the Lord's messenger called out to him for the heavens and said.. . ."

At the apparent urging of God, at the very last moment before the axe is about to fall, God forbids the offing – or should I say offering – of Isaac in sacrifice. And, well then, off they go, back home, ostensibly back to Sarah, back home. But there is no narrative in this passage to describe their return to her. None. Thus we hear nothing about how Sarah might have reacted at being told about their 'adventure'.

And Sarah says nothing. And that's It???

All we hear from or about Sarah is in the following chapter:

> CHAPTER 23: *"And Sarah's life was a hundred and twenty-seven years, the years of Sarah's life."*

According to words of the text we have in *Torah,* we do not know, by Sarah's words or actions, how she reacted when Abraham, or Isaac, when, or if, they told her about what they had almost done. Sarah's reactions in her words or actions are not part of the text. We have no inkling as to Sarah's reactions in her own words in this portion of *Torah*. The *Akedah* was to become the pivotal passage in Jewish lives and hearts. The *Akedah* burrows deeply into the consciousness and future actions of most Jews. It is the keynote story about **sacrifice** in Jewish lives. The *Akedah* will be in the back of most Jewish minds when it comes to reading Jewish history. The *Akedah* will appear in Jewish family lives if errant Jewish offspring wander from Jewish parents. The *Akedah*, by its ubiquity during the High Holy Days, may be the single most important *Torah* portion.

Looks like the only claim to Matriarchy that Sarah gets credit for is that of becoming a mother to a boy-child when she had been considered to be too-old to conceive.

So. We are charged with the duty to engage with *Torah*. And, as a conscientious newcomer, and thus I pledged by the side of my own mikvah a dozen years ago, I made my commitment to study. It's 2025 and I turn to study the *Akedah* yet again. So, here I am today, shuffling reference books and articles and my own random notes, flitting this way and that way in the noble writings of my esteemed predecessors, the wise men of the ages with their commentaries. I have dipped into their mindful thinking during all these passing years. And this season of 2025, I refer to with greater attention, a book on my shelves whose clean unwrinkled pages reveal my neglect: ***The Bible With Sources Revealed* by Richard Elliott Friedman**.

What I discover from Friedman's book is the **Documentary Hypothesis**. In it Friedman clearly presents possible sources and the history of the words in our scripture — in this case in *Torah*. Friedman quotes from Robert Alter:

> *"A few brief remarks about the structure of* ***Genesis as a book*** *are in order. Genesis comprises* ***two large literary units—the Primeval History and the Patriarchal Tales.*** *The two differ not only in subject but to some extent in style and perspective."*
>
> *— Robert Alter*

In other words, later editors — called Redactors — were early authors of Jewish history, culture, and observances. They were men and they may have felt it their duty to define Jewish life and to define, within the text of what will become

Jewish scripture, how to live a most observant Jewish life.

Well, and it is no very great surprise, most of the authors, editors, and Redactors of *Torah* were men. And, of course, most of the earliest Talmudic — the *Talmud* being an ongoing source of commentary for existing *Torah* — and the commentators were men as well.

Lately, I dipped back into the *Torah*, actual, to review the story of the Binding of Isaac, called the *Akedah*. And something feels different to me this time. So, as my go-to source, I open two volumes of the *Encyclopaedia Judaica*.

I consult my *Encyclopaedia Judaica Vol. 2 A-Ang, page 482*. In it I find:

"The Akedah influenced both Christian and Islamic thought . . . **The Akedah to the moralists was a fertile text for the inculcation of religious and ethical values**. . ."

How on Earth do we speak in our sacred literature? How do words communicate? Well, first of all, we communicate using words. The choices of words count in the first lines of communication. But there are other ways we communicate as well. One way of communication that I would like to focus on in the *Akedah* is pauses or silences or omissions. In particular to the *Akedah*, it is omissions I would focus on during my study sessions on this particular set of High Holy Days here in 2025.

It would be helpful if we could each open our books to

Genesis 22:1-19 and *Genesis 23*. Look if you will and note the absences and omissions. Omissions imply the work of one group of writers to omit the words of another group of writers. Editors, we could call them. And according to ***The Bible With Sources Revealed*** **by Richard Elliott Friedman** that is exactly what Friedman calls these earliest editors of *Torah*. Friedman refers to them as Redactors. They are those who edit or remove existing text.

Absences of words in narratives may depend upon editors, who may remove portions of existing text. I may prefer absences to be more accidental or unintended than specific omissions. I may, or may not, call omissions: careless or intentional, or, if I am feeling more critical: venal.

In addition, and I mean no criticism, shouldn't a First Matriarch, as Sarah is so-called, have left behind her own words, a guidebook so to speak, of rules and regulations for women in particular to study and to take to heart as we move through our lives? There are no words from Sarah. First Matriarch or otherwise, she leaves us with nothing resembling *do's* or *don'ts*. Sarah's tongue was bound. She uttered no commentary on the events or narrative in the chapter about the Binding of Isaac, the Akedah.

In light of this omission, consider this as well: among those who determined which statements in *Torah* are deemed to be *commandments*, Maimonides stated that there are 613 commandments found in *Torah*. There are 248 positive commandments (do's) and 365 negative commandments (don'ts). Not one of these is advice from Sarah.

Looks like the only claim to Matriarchy that Sarah gets credit for is that of becoming a mother to a boy-child when she had been considered to be too-old to conceive.

If the intentions of its authors were to instruct women in future generations, it is sadly missing in this chapter of *Torah*, called the Binding of Isaac or the Akedah. Blank. Muffled. Stifled? Sarah's stories, narratives about Sarah, spoken words in which she might have included advice for us, we women of the distant future of Judaism – there is nothing there for us who listen for these kinds of things from Sarah – her words, her in-person narratives – but we find nothing. The tongue of Sarah is bound in the Akedah.

The *Akedah,* therefore, is not a narrative about the Binding of Isaac. It is the narrative, surely more accurate, that is about the Binding of Sarah's Tongue. The Binding of Sarah's Speech. The *Akedah* might be better named: The Binding of Sarah. This is my midrash after reading, yet again, *Genesis 22*.

Today I am sitting here with a group of my women friends. Seated here for lunch, we have dubbed our gathering our Talking Table. Yet, unlike Sarah, the women here have reclaimed, have asserted, our own voices. We share our own stories. Rather I should say: We share our own speech. Thus we give birth sharing our own life stories. Late in life, now in our elder years, and now, with full consciousness of the fact that we had had to struggle to get our voices heard and stories told, and on the table, so to speak, for all to hear — now, finally, we tell and retell our stories in our own voices — tongues unbound — and it is balm to heal us after so very many years of being stifled, muffled, or silently ignored. Women's stories have been bound in silence for generations. And so when we read Sarah's last story about what Abraham almost did to Isaac and when we review this story over and over again during every subsequent High Holy Day season, the title that we are most accustomed to is: *The Binding of Isaac.* And it is about sacrifice in Jewish lives.

But upon further study, it is clear to see that it is, instead, very much more surely, it is *The Binding of Sarah.*

This sliver of midrash provides a portal through which you, dear reader, may push either way: agree or disagree. I wonder, now after creating this midrash, if I am not perhaps somewhat personally related to Sarah, a soulmate at the very least, if not her cousin. I was drawn to, and infuriated by, Sarah's portion of *Torah*, distinguished as she is, even now, as one of the Matriarchs of my chosen Jewish life. What could have so moved me to such feelings? I wonder if it were not that at least some part of my own story, of my eighty years, resounds through my reading about Sarah?

I am not a rabbi, but: The message of the *Akedah,* deeply buried within the context, the very structure, of that familiar text of this *Torah* portion — to future women who have stories — the message is that there may be in the future, and that, sadly, inevitably, there will be, *The Binding of Women's Tongues.*

Amen.

BUT, I Have a Friend Who IS

What if I'm wrong. What if I have gone off the deep end with my midrash, my own take on this passage in *Torah* which is entitled The Binding of Isaac or the Akedah. What if I am simply wrong to conclude that this *Torah* portion should be renamed as: The Binding of Sarah? Or The Binding of Women's Tongues? What if my midrash crumbles into the question: The Binding of What and by Whom?

For this manuscript, I asked four friends to do the dreaded 'first-reader' task. Which is to take a copy of my rough and ready 'book', and read it through with an eye to what? To evaluation? To tweaks? To obvious things I missed and that they, first readers, need to read about in order to clarify or to flesh something out? First readers need to know that, whatever they say, we will still be friends at the end of their critique, opinion, raspberry, thumbs up, or thumbs down. It takes several tries to find the kind of first-reader who can take the pressure and not just flatter me that I am 'just so talented' and so on and on and on, just to keep my friendship. I hope I am a better person than that.

But sitting in the first-reader seat, it's a fearsome prospect to tell your friend, me the writer, that something is wrong with her manuscript. Flattery gets you nowhere as the beleaguered first-reader. I now have four such brave friends that I have winnowed down from several others. Trusted. Discerning readers. And brave.

One such trusted first-reader is Rabbi Deborah Brin. I have studied *Torah* with her in many of her classes over many years. She encouraged me to write my first Jewish-themed book, *A Non-Swimmer Considers Her Mikvah*. Her words of encouragement to me for my telling the story of how I became Jewish after age fifty went like this:

"This book will open doors for you."

As indeed it has. Subsequently, this rabbi has also been a first-reader for my novels.

So I asked her if she would have the time or the inclination to read this, my latest book, my memoir. This book you hold, dear reader.

Here's how Rabbi Brin's summary of her first-reading of this manuscript proceeded upon my handing her these 245 pages for her review. I said to her,

"I am fraught with misgivings and hesitations about actually going to print."

She replied,

"Not to keep you on pins and needles. I liked your message

a lot. Keep breathing and believe in yourself."

Then, when we sat down together with her copy of the manuscript, she said, "It's not a midrash."

Arghhhhh. What? What? This was scary to hear.

Then she continued,

"It's Commentary."

"But, Rabbi, isn't commentary the product of all of the wise minds down through the centuries — Maimonides, Rashi, and so forth. All those guys. Aren't they the ones who carry the honor of their work and their thinking and are entitled to have their work called Commentary?"

And she responded,

"No, it's not just them. But what you have done here with all of your examples that you narrate throughout this book with your examples of how we communicate, how on Earth we speak, all from your own life. It's how you discuss and relate all of these experiences back to your original take on the Binding of Isaac, the Akedah, and Sarah. Your book here goes beyond the text in *Torah*. Beyond midrash. Midrash usually reads like a narrative. I see yours as Commentary, not midrash. You go on to consider broader ideas and questions about the text. Your book, this book, is Commentary."

I had had the naive notion that only the works of distant past wise Jewish thinkers, rabbis, and philosophers, could attain to the honor of commentary. That some of my ideas and explorations that I turn and turn in my analysis of this *Torah* portion could attain to being called 'Commentary' raised this book up in my humble estimation. I kvel!

Commentary departs time and text to explore distant ideas, far distant places, distant times in the future perhaps. From, let's posit, the destruction of the Second Temple right up to and including 2025. Midrash stays within the boundaries of text. Commentary goes far beyond time itself and history, yet launches from text.

Now, from this point forward, and much thanks to my friend and first reader, a rabbi of many dozens of years, I shall refer to her honorific, this book, my memoir, as my Commentary – cap. C – based upon my life stories and my take on this world I occupy. With all my years, I come to contemplate: How on Earth do we speak?

Is it generations of silenced women that drive our quest, within scripture, to find substantial and perhaps brand new meaning, or even to discover advice or inspiration from other historic female figures in scripture – does the study of our books yield solutions or advice about how we, 21st Century women, should speak? And, most importantly, when we question scripture, are we to be criticized? We know that, as students of *Torah*, it is incumbent upon us students to question and to speak up. So who cares how we debate a passage in *Torah?*

Here is Commentary from Rabbi Shimon bar Yochal, from his Second-Century teachings in *Sefer Ha Zohar, Bamidbar 152a:*

If the contents of the Torah were meant to be taken literally,
you and I could have composed a much better book.
But if it is indeed inspired by the Creator,
then just as God is infinite, so is the ***word of God*** *infinite,*
imbued with meanings that transcend any
one particular interpretation.
It is upon us . . . to drink from it . . . as from an eternal
wellspring, and to find ever-fresh meaning in it for each
of our life situations . . .
stay with it, dialogue with it, wrestle with it until it unfolds
meaning for you personally, until it reveals its mystery.

A Nudge of Jewish Humor

We may debate this if you like. We are actually allowed to debate with *Torah.* It is somewhat incumbent upon our Jewish selves to argue with any and every thing we study in our books. We may present our own commentaries and midrashim and mythos and metaphor, meld all of these as we study *Torah.* We may also argue infinitely about this. Three Jews, Five Opinions. But, in the end, this is our way to study. This is how we engage with scripture and with *Torah.* Talmudic, and much other rabbinic commentary down through the centuries, exists for every chapter and verse and even for dozens of single words found in our most sacred studies. But does all of our engagement, questioning, theorizing, or even of doubt as we create midrash — does all of this dissuade us further from being Jewish? Does all this drive us away from our Jewish selves?

This is the stuff of Jewish humor. Witness this classic: *"Two Rabbis argue late into the night about the existence of God and, using strong arguments from the scriptures, ended up indisputably disproving His existence. The next day, one Rabbi was surprised to see the other walking into shul for morning services."I thought we had agreed there was no God," he said."Yes, but what does that have to do with it?" replied the other.*

Yes. What do all these words and omissions of words have to do with any of it? Next year we will study the *Akedah* yet again, walking into shul yet again.

My commentary on the *Akedah* posits that Sarah's voice and her stories and her narratives in that portion of the Torah had been stifled — removed? — *intentionally or unintendedly* as the *Al Chet* warns us. Mistakes or sins created with or without words are equally culpable in their power to cause harm. Sarah's words and actions may be simply lost or, perhaps, never included in the first place or removed by Redactors. Sarah's voice, her ruminations, her conversations, or her inward reflections and thoughts, Sarah's entire story and voice, in its own utterances, were absolutely not included within the text that is presented as her story in the *Akedah*. It's so paltry. It's so blank. It is only relayed in a cool voice, cold almost, tone and manner. Sarah's part in the Binding of Isaac portion is missing from

> *Does all of our engagement, questioning, theorizing, or even of doubt within Torah as we create Commentary — does all of this dissuade us further from being Jewish?.*

the narrative. Her feelings or potential words are missing. Thrown away? What on Earth transpired between Sarah after Abraham and Isaac returned?

I do not shrink from asking: And then she died? That's it?

Memories Commence

Yet there is something else about my *Torah* studies lately. More specifically: there is something mysterious that happens with my studies, now that I am nearing my eighth decade. Well, perhaps 'mysterious' is too woo-woo. What I mean, more precisely, there is an unexpected and powerful process that affects how my memory works its way through these so many decades on Earth. I currently retrieve numerous, very many in fact, entire conversations and events that I now see quite differently than when I first experienced them.

Conversations, for example, with my parents wherein their intended communication was well understood by me, back then. But wherein, afterwards, I responded with nothing. Not a word from me in response to them. But wherein I now remember how I felt and how I could have responded, but did not respond. So there I sat, wordless but not uncomprehending. I feel that part of my lack of response to parental words was as protection. If I said nothing in response then the words could never escalate into hard words or angry backing and forthing and some part of me — especially after, say, age thirteen – some new part of me withdrew and stayed silent and thus, maintained, a secretive part of my actions from teen years onward. And this, this, is what I now look back on several occasions from then onward, where I kept to myself. Stayed silent. Bound my own tongue.

Ha! So then, not unlike Sarah during the narrative of the Akedah. Ha! No wonder my reaction to this scriptural story was so pointed, angry, probing. It's no wonder I wrestled with a fitting midrash – at least as far as my own deeply silent nature – to focus upon the silence of the narrative about Sarah. Sarah's tongue was bound. So, too, mine had been.

Sarah's tongue was bound. So, too, mine had been.

It's no wonder we glom onto whatever it is in our scripture that speaks most clearly to our own selves. This is very interesting. And a worthy note for further study, I do believe. Hold this in mind – my midrash and the memories that it evokes.

How on Earth?

So, perhaps you ask:

"You took to your mikvah at a fair ripe age. How'd that ever happen?"

Well, to quote from my first Jewish-themed book, *A Non-Swimmer Considers Her Mikvah,* WINNER 2016 New Mexico-Arizona Book Awards, my memoir of events that led up to my mikvah. From page 88, here is an excerpt:

> *"If it is imaginable to have been somewhat Jewish by default, I can honestly say that I have never missed a single yahrzeit for my mother's death,*
> *September 30, 1968"*

She was forty-six.

It was not only imaginable, it was a fact. I was already, in some ways, acting Jewishly by intuition and with intention.

I observed my mother's yahrzeits, year after year, long before I even knew what a yahrzeit was. Later I discover that being Jewish is not about belief, it is about action.

I did not simply believe in a yahrzeit observance – I did not even know what the word meant. I had not even heard of the word.

I was making yahrzeit.

Yahrzeit was already instinctively a part of my being, of my psyche, long before I learned the word yahrzeit. There may have even been an element in my thinking that I had invented this little ceremonial observance, all on my own, instinctively.

I was already giving life to my first Jewish actions.

I made my first yahrzeit for my mother on September 30, 1969. My father did not call me on that date. He never called. He never, ever again, referred to that date of September 30, 1968.

In addition to my burgeoning Jewish actions after my

mother's death, there is this earlier influence that she had on my thinking. Here is another excerpt from my book *A Non-Swimmer Considers Her Mikvah:*

> *"The most important question I ever asked her was . . . But Mama, what about all the Hindus and the Buddhists and all the people in China who might be good people, living good lives – will they burn in hell if they do not accept Christian doctrine? . . .*
>
> *She looked me straight in the eyes, her beautiful and intense brown eyes fixing on mine, serious and compelling, and said to me: "No. They will not burn in hell if they are not Christians. It doesn't work that way."*

What an extraordinary gift from my own mother. When I was seventeen, she mindfully bequeathed to me a conclusion about one religion that opened my mind forever after. I never attended another church service after that day. But I began a lifetime of reading and talking and listening to what a universe of others believed as truth, or myth, or supposition, or doctrine. The Buddha. Bertrand Russell. Freud. Jung. Iyengar. Zen. Existentialism. Nihilism. All of it, and all of them, and more of them, I cannot even recall.

What an extraordinary gift from my own mother.

Then, when I was too old, perhaps, to read more, to think

more, to ponder the great imponderables, I signed up for a Jewish silent meditation retreat in 1996 led by Rabbi David Cooper and I wrote my first midrash based on that week's *Torah* portion and read it aloud to the whole group who was on retreat:

Quote from the *Torah* Portion of that week:

Parsha Re'Eh: Devarim – Deuteronomy – Chapter 14:29

". . . the stranger, and the orphan, and the widow, who are inside your gates, shall come, and shall eat and be satisfied . . ."

My first midrash prepared in 1996 which reads:

"I am somewhat a stranger – a metaphorical orphan – when it comes to navigating a mystical and spiritual path. I realized on Thursday – for the first time in my 50 years – that not a single person in my family or my husband's family has taken this route. Well – one odd maternal uncle, but he liked Wagnerian Operas too.

(At this point I received mild good-natured chuckles from fellow students)

Nevertheless – here I trek. Thank you for taking me – the orphan – inside your gates to eat and be satisfied."

And, thus, with my poor aging brain crammed with much back-story, so to speak, with this background 'noise' to my further narrative arc, I began to listen more mindfully than I had previously been able. I began to study for my mikvah.

I took it all in and I do believe I digested it well and mindfully, and there I stood, decades later, facing the clear deep waters of my mikvah in the year 2011.

My Jewish self was already with me on that day and had been since my birth in October, 1945:

Torah Portion on that day: Lech L'echa:

"Go from your land, from your birthplace and from your father's house, to the land which I will show you."

Providential? Well, yes, if you hold with such things. Coincidental? Yes, more likely. Correlation leading to eventuality? Well, probably not. After all, wiser men than I posit that 'correlation is not causation'.

Aunt Bea

In the Jewish tradition — or rather I could sometimes call it: Jewish Notions — it is not advisable to proselytize. It is, in fact, completely Ill-Advisable. And even very secular Jews, do not try to convince anybody to join the tribe. Thus, after I attended a ten day Jewish silent meditation retreat in 1996 led by Rabbi David Cooper and his wife Shoshona I had begun to think that I would like to begin my studies. Now you may ask: how can a Jewish retreat be **silent**? Well, with about a hundred attendees, four of them were Rabbis. So go figure. The program included daily readings from *Torah* and on the Friday afternoon we participants were asked to do midrash on that week's portion. It was the only time we were allowed to speak in the entire retreat. I was surprised and a little embarrassed when, after presenting my midrash, reading it aloud, there was a stirring of legs and feet after my reading. Later I learned that within services it is not okay to applaud, but if a speaker does a worthy midrash, the audience will stir in approval. I was pleased and touched and my decision to join the tribe was now set in my mind and heart.

Bea paused, perhaps took a tiny sip of wine, set the glass back on the counter and responded: "Think of the Food!"

It was shortly after returning from that retreat that we had our Aunt Bea out for a visit. 1996.

We were in the kitchen. I was chopping onions and grating cheese. Bea was seated on 'her' stool at the counter, watching me prepare dinner. We both had a small glass of white wine for company. As I was working, I asked her:

"What would you think if I started studying with a Rabbi?"

Bea paused, perhaps took a tiny sip of wine, set the glass back on the counter and responded:

"Think of the Food!"

I loved her answer. It was so, well, as you see, it was just right according to tradition yet was so positive as to her approval.

We had such lovely talks every morning. Bea would always bring us matching Lanz flannel nightgowns and there we'd sit on the sofa with our cups of coffee talking. Just talking.

I painted her portrait wearing her flannel nightie, and placed a candelabrum in the corner and called the picture: Candle Unburn.

After a few months of painting portraits of friends and self, I was given a show at my alma mater in 1998. The gallery for the paintings was in what had been one of the painting studios when I was an undergraduate. Almost every person I painted came to the reception. Including Aunt Bea. And it was fun photographing each person next to their portraits. Everybody was happy and laughing with my interpretations of each of them and they all gushed over their pictures. Except Aunt Bea.

She later told Gary she hated her portrait. That it was demeaning in her nightgown.

I was hurt. Not completely crushed. But definitely hurt. To me it represented the very best of our relationship. To Bea it was insulting.

It did not end our relationship. But it put a pause on how she viewed my work as a painter. We managed to let it rest. Put her feelings to one side and mine to the other side. And we continued our talks.

Then, after a couple of years, during the time of the Holy Days — very near Yom Kippur — I went down to LA to visit Bea. We decided to go to our favorite Deli and dine on Matzahball soup and chopped liver. We were having a wonderful time, chomping and slurping and it was a bright sunny LA Day.

Then I noticed Bea getting a serious posture. She peered into her soup. Took another small bite of bread and chopped liver and began to speak. As she was finding her voice, tone manner and subject, she placed her right hand against her chest.

“Remember that painting you did of me? That portrait?”

“Yes, Bea. I do. You didn’t like it as I recall.”

“Well. I think if I saw it now I would feel different.”

I noticed she was gently tapping her heart. Tap. Tap. Tap.

“And I think if I saw it now I would like it.” Tap. Tap.

There she was, making amends, right there over the Matzahballs.

There is one other significant event, a single word only, that pressed me further in my aim to become Jewish. Duke. This was the nickname that a rabbi used repeatedly during his talk at the Bima for Gary’s Uncle Martin’s funeral. He said it several times. Gary and I whispered, in mock confusion: ‘are we in the wrong funeral?’ Turned out it was an honest if fumbling mistake on the rabbi’s part. He had misinterpreted

Uncle Martin's college football team nickname. Well. What I said to Gary afterward: "I want to become Jewish and get to know a rabbi well enough so that he calls me by my REAL name when I'm dead."

My Mother the Gunnery Instructor

My mother was a Gunnery Instructor in the U.S. Navy during World War Two.

Imagine if you will, a recent college graduate in 1942. She is from a family of brothers. Dominant lads, one much older, one much younger. But competitive types, very smart, very smart-alecky. Prime candidates for being drafted in the continuing conflicts in Europe. Of course, she did not have this worry, but nonetheless she had internalized a nudging variety of patriotism and sense of duty. Her father an engineer. Her mother a poet. Both of them strong opinioned older parents. Lots of talk at table about the Depression and FDR and war.

My mother's surname was Jewish. Or could have been. I spent many hours touring *ancestry.com* searching for clues to her father's origins and grandfather's travels to the United States in 1848. So how on earth did she land as a Gunnery Instructor in the U. S. Navy in 1943? The world was still at war back then, still raging, unresolved, pre-atomic bombs. How on Earth had she learned – did she indeed need to learn? – her skills with arms? How on Earth did my mother separate into neat compartments politics and killing and love and, pretty soon, childbirth? And how on Earth did she speak about this period of her life? I inherited my mother's keen ear for nuance, for words that reveal secrets or pauses that disguise them and for words that parse meanings of ideas like ethics and mythology.

My mother was a Gunnery Instructor. She never spoke about it. She was a sharp shooter. She was best in her nascent class who studied gunnery at Hunter College, right in the thick of the war that would be named World War Two. Even back then in those urgent circumstances the 'girls' in her class posed with some training weapons alongside the Hunter College's School of Mortuary Science signage. It was their girlish joke. Their sense of humor. I didn't get it until I was much older.

She taught nascent young soldiers the craft, the stealth, the unblinking focus of the eyes and of the mind. She worked to prepare and to arm these little men for their future postings that would require aviation gunnery. They would live or die by her instruction. They would shoot weapons, aimed well, at distant and moving metal aircraft or even at entire hometowns down below, way over there or way down there, but not filled with other human souls — surely not. Not so you'd notice, you, a serious trained soldier. That was not part of the curriculum for air to air gunnery. Most likely they would die, or parts of them would die, even if they came home alive and in one piece after battles abroad. They would die, though alive, dead inside and they wouldn't even know it. Dead yet no longer living, those students of my mother's gunnery instruction. Speaking not of the unspeakable.

She was a sharp-shooter. She was best in her class a potential Officer Candidate.

QUALIFICATIONS FOR SEPCIALIST (G)

AVIATION FREE GUNNERY INSTRUCTOR SECOND CLASS

PRACTICAL FACTORS RANGE FIRING.

Demonstrate facility in the proper firing of a shot gun, a service pistol, machine gun, and turret machine gun. Demonstrate a thorough knowledge of the kinds and causes of stoppages and malfunctions, and demonstrate skill in correcting them. Demonstrate ability to place the range crew and to organize a small group of students for firing. Demonstrate thorough knowledge of range procedures and safety precautions. 1/30/45 CPO.

Then again, and of course, given wartime and the short uniform skirts by designer Mainbocher and the romance of all that danger and uncertainty and the weaponry and you could die on your next mission, my mother fell in love and married a handsome Royal Air Force Pilot who had been stationed during a top-secret mission devised by our President and Britain's Prime Minister. My father was posted for a while in the United States at Pensacola Florida Air Force Base in 1943. Scant documentation of this mission is contained in the six years of recorded military records I obtained from the Royal Air Force after his death. Buried deep in the personal remembrance of another pilot of that era it is stated that:

"The hard-earned Solid Silver Wings of the U.S. Navy Air Corps that we proudly wore on the right breast of our tunics along with . . . our Royal Air Force Wings on the left."

I have a single photograph of both sets of wings on my father's RAF uniform as he stood for photographs after his wedding to my mother in 1944.

And there she was, tall and powerful and great long legs highlighted by fetching bows on her uniform's Navy shoes, casual, young, engaged in world events, not shy, not simpering, solidly there, in her Mainbocher skirt.

They married during a short leave taken in New York and, surprise, surprise, my mother got pregnant with what would turn out to be me.

Confidential

Medical Department

Subj: M. Z. Sp (G)

Physical examination on subject named member of the Women's Reserve disclosed the existence of early pregnancy. This has been confirmed by an Aschheim-Zondek Test, which was reported positive.

She had a touch of laryngitis too, back then. For a few days she could barely speak to lead her gunnery classes. The doctor kidded her with a comment that she repeated, jokingly, in a later letter to *The Pilot*:

The doctor said: "A last: A woman who can't talk!"

During that period of WWII the U.S. Navy did not know what to do with pregnant gunnery instructors so my mother was:

". . . discharged from U.S. Naval Air Station . . . and the U.S. Naval Service UNDER HONORABLE CONDITIONS . . . Dated this 12th day of March, 1945"

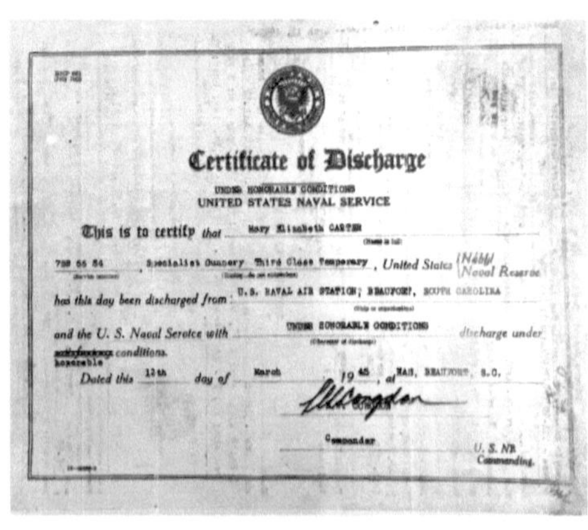

Certificate of Discharge

UNDER HONORABLE CONDITIONS

UNITED STATES NAVAL SERVICE

This is to certify that Mary Elizabeth CARTER

(Name in full)

798 66 84, Specialist Gunnery Third Class Temporary, United States Naval Reserve

has this day been discharged from U.S. NAVAL AIR STATION, BEAUFORT, SOUTH CAROLINA

and the U. S. Naval Service with UNDER HONORABLE CONDITIONS discharge under honorable conditions.

Dated this 12th day of March 1945, at NAS, BEAUFORT, S.C.

Commander

U. S. NR

Commanding.

About a million years later, when we were all approaching our 80s, a friend of ours who had served as a Green Beret in Vietnam for several years listened to me joking about something my mother used to say. She said it enough, in fact, that I have always remembered it. My mother, the former U.S. Navy Gunnery Instructor, used to always say that if anybody hurt me she would kill them. And my response, shocked and disbelieving:

"But Mama, you'd be sent to jail for murder."

"It would have been worth it to have protected you."

Later, decades later, a half century after my mother's death, our Green Beret friend asked me:

"Your mother could have killed somebody at one hundred yards and nobody would ever have caught her."

"Did your mother ever tell you anything about what she did as a Gunnery instructor? Weaponry? Or any of the training classes she conducted?"

No, I answered, truthfully:

"She never said a single thing to me about when she taught gunnery in the U.S. Navy. She only ever said that she would kill anybody who hurt me."

May 1944

"Dear Mom, . . . I can now strip a 30. Caliber machine gun – know how to operate a turret and guns contained in it. Can recognize in about 1/25th of a second 5 Jap planes,

1 German, and 1 English; shoot a pistol and 12 gauge shot gun, run a trap house — compute various sighting problems — name advantages and disadvantages of various iron sights, telescopic sights and reflector sights . . ."

Then our friend, the former Green Beret, put his big old arm around my neck and said:

"Your mother could have killed somebody at one hundred yards and nobody would ever have caught her."

Secondary Familial PTSD

The newlyweds would be separated for 18 months during which time they wrote almost daily. My mother never knew where her handsome husband was stationed. Her anxiety about his survival was ruefully monitored by Britain's Royal Air Force. All of her letters were to be sent to a central RAF base, then forwarded onward to wherever he was stationed. She launched her love letters across the dark Atlantic from Reseda California, off to who-knows-where.

Here is a letter I wrote to the editors of the *London Review of Books* that was posted, in print, following my own take on one of their book reviews:

> *"Julia Laite writes about the effects of 'Dear John' letters on soldiers' mental health, and the consequences for the women who wrote them — LRB 10 February 2022. Both my parents were in the military during the Second World War. My mother joined the US navy in 1943 and became an instructor. My father was British, conscripted in 1939 for the duration. He was in the Royal Air Force for*

six years, becoming a flight sergeant and pilot. They met when my father was on a training mission on a US navy airbase in Pensacola, Florida, and were married wearing their dress uniforms in New York in 1944. They were 22 years old.

My father was subsequently transferred back to the European theatre, and then, after the war, to India. He was bound to be, for the duration, a stranger in a strange land. He was gone for eighteen months. Before he left, my mother got pregnant with me. She was given an honorable discharge and went home to her mother's small ranch in Southern California.

> *Poor child-mother and child-father and their demanding, wiggly baby-child, alone in orange grove, dirt-road Reseda.*

During their separation, my parents wrote letters back and forth almost every day. Neither of them ever mentioned where he was. Her letters were filled with enthusiasm and buck-up cheer, as in the ads she may have seen in Life magazine at that time.

I was born in October 1945. My father wasn't demobilized until I was nearly a year old. He was, if not shell-shocked, certainly numbed and slightly crazy from the war. He went 'home' to my mother and me, a stranger in a strange land. By the time he got to the San Fernando Valley,

I was a willful toddler. When my grandmother put me in his arms, he took hold of me awkwardly, reluctantly, as I shrieked, squirmed and shat. Then he handed me back. My grandmother never forgave him. Pretty soon, she kicked all three of us out of her house — the pilot, my mother and me. Poor child-mother and child-father and their demanding, wiggly baby-child, alone in orange grove, dirt-road Reseda. All they had, my parents, aside from me, were their military uniforms and arm patches, citizen soldiers now, both of them.

My point in telling this story is to register another form of mental stress and potentially deep psychological damage done to some Second World War vets who returned, physically well but emotionally damaged, and sadly distant from babies they had never had a chance to bond with. I call it secondary familial PTSD. I observed it as I grew up, as did many of my friends. They had the same framed photographs on top of their TVs: their parents' weddings, all the men in uniform."

Near Miss in a Cessna

This is the story of a near miss in a Cessna. Not this Cessna. The one above. But one very like it in body configuration. Yellow fuselage. Silver wings, fabric stretched over the superstructure of the wings, then stretched, held taught, by silver paint called dope. Doping it was called and the silver dope would dry very hard and solid over the structure of the wings. Just the way an artist would stretch canvas over a frame. The paint dries and forms a solid body for a painting. But by the time this next episode takes place, we had bought and sold several larger Cessnas. At the moment of the following event, we owned a four-seater.

What happened in and around that little craft on an afternoon in 1967? It was just a few weeks before my college graduation. It will take forty-five years for me to navigate the circumstances of that flight. Throughout my childhood, we flew all over the country in our own Cessnas. Different crafts as I got too large to lodge in the luggage area of the smaller planes. So by the time I was in college, my parents were flying all over in our latest and largest Cessnas. There was nothing unusual about our travels and never anything dangerous. Until I discovered this event that unfolded in my consciousness over several decades.

It is Spring. 1967. I sit, crosswise on my dorm bed, studying for a final exam, thumbing, desultory, through Jansen's *History of Art*. In four weeks, I, clad in black silk, will claim my scroll, my new identity: Bachelor of Art.

"What are we going to do now, Mary Carter?"

The dorm echoes the sounds of finals week. Up and down the halls [illegible] giggles, doors slamming, slippers scuffing, coffee cups clinking. Chanting is heard: algebraic equations, lists of flora and fauna, mumblings, sighs of despair. The phone rings. It's for you, Mary.

"Mama?"

"Are you okay? Where are you? Are you okay?"

It is that tone of voice every daughter knows and every daughter's mother employs when something is wrong, wrong, just plain wrong.

"I'm fine, Mama. I'm studying for art history. The final is tomorrow."

"Are you okay?"

"Yes, I'm fine, Mama. Fine. What? What is it?"

Nothing. My mother takes a breath, continues in a calmer tone, anodyne comments about turbulent weather on the way home from a short hop up the Owens Valley. Love and love you, signing off, good luck on your exam tomorrow. Click.

A few months later my mother mentions, off the cuff:

“We experienced some heavy turbulence on the way home through the Owens Valley.”

Nothing more. Subject closed. In a few months she will lie in her bed, diagnosis certain, “eight months’ max”, quipped the chatty doctor.

There were more important things to worry about than a little turbulence back in ’67.

Once or twice in the intervening years, my father mentions, casual, in passing, that he put the Cessna into a spin. He told me the plane had risen in elevation to where they would not have been able to breathe. The little plane had no oxygen capabilities or equipment. He forced the plane way down in elevation by putting it into a spin. I think I heard it as “a tail spin”, but I am not sure. He said the weather condition that created those sudden updrafts was indicated by lenticular cloud formations. There had not been any lenticular clouds upon takeoff. After the near-miss, they flew home, just like that, really low and really slow. Nothing more. No details. Certainly, no dramatics.

The next thing I hear about that flight home was in 2012. My father by then was fading in and out of Alzheimer’s time — skipping from one episode to another, back and forth in time and in attention. He says to me:

"Remember that flight home from the Owens Valley?"

"Yeah. Hey, what happened?"

"We opened the cockpit doors."

And then he was gone, off again with his scattered attention, onto something else and I could not persuade him to get back to the topic and to speak further about that flight.

By serendipitous coincidence, around 2012 I had discovered a long-ago colleague of mine from my years at Grey Advertising. Doug and I were emailing back and forth about our lives for the past forty years. He had gotten his private pilot's license and had had a Cessna for many years. I asked him about the weather conditions in Owens Valley and if he knew anything about those harbingers of pending danger for Cessna pilots, lenticular clouds. He did indeed know. He had had the same experience that my father had mentioned and he felt it was sheer luck that he, Doug, had made it back alive. And since my parents had survived, Doug guessed that my father had had very special training in the Royal Air Force about handling planes that were in extreme dangers of all kinds. My father had been a pilot in the RAF for six years during WWII.

Then I asked Doug what he thought my father had meant when he said:

"We opened the cockpit doors."

Doug responded instantly:

"They thought they were going down."

"How do you know that, Doug?"

"When a pilot of a small craft sees that it will crash, he opens the cockpit doors so that, if they crash, and the craft rolls on the ground, there will be a way out. They thought they were going down."

"We opened the cockpit doors."

My parents never told me that. All I got was hints and obfuscation from them. Neither of them told me much at all about that dangerous flight. To think: if they had gone down, they would have died just a few days before my college graduation. Turned out, our little family went down anyway. Not with lenticular cloud warnings, yet there were other threats and dangers. My mother died in 1968. Age forty-six. My father went into a tail spin and crash-landed somewhere but his doors were shut that time around.

Flight Cap

Remember when we flew all over the place?

My father has a cap, a flying talisman perhaps, a beat up somewhat threadbare black wool baseball style hat. The bill of this cap has been folded so many times, jammed into so many pants pockets, tugged at so diligently, that all of the stiffness has gone out of it. At the crown there is a permanent crease that extends from what would be eartop to eartop. The underside of the bill — which at one time might have been yellow and at this point is a very faded grubby beige — has thick faded black letters on it: Nicky. Nicky?

My father is never without his cap as we fly cross country in our little Cessnas.

The Royal Air Force taught my father how to fly lumbering deafening PBYs and he continues flying lessons after WWII out at a little ragtag air field in the San Fernando Valley which we called Coffin Field. Actually it was called the Whiteman Air Field, but we called it Coffin Field in honor of the man who ran the place: Hank Coffin. He was an old school, crop dusting pilot, more dust than crop in those days. Hanky, as he is dubbed by the plane owners who tie down out here, is a jovial red-faced type. It's a good idea to be jovial when your last name is Coffin and you oversee about fifty small plane tie-downs, an aviation gas pump and two slumping aircraft hangars. Hanky presides over his flying kingdom from a low-roofed ratty flight shack. At his desk, he teeters backward on a murderously defective swivel chair. The screeching back and arms of this wreck tilt so far back that Hanky looks like he might launch straight upward into the clouds of the nicotine smoked ceiling. His desk is stacked — although stacked implies some form of order; there was none at that desk — it is, rather, slung, strewn and encrusted with ragged flight plan folders, creased aviator's maps, wadded candy wrappers,

It's a good idea to be jovial when your last name is Coffin and you oversee about fifty small plane tie-downs.

coffee-stained paper cups, aged and reeking cigarette butts, chewed up useless ball point pens and oily wires and engine parts; a place for everything and everything in its place.

The air strip is gravely and just about adequately paved, a narrow runway, with tarmac, that lines up dead-reckoning with three towering smoke stacks at the far end. At takeoff the little planes – Cessnas, Stinsons, Aeroncas, and Beechcraft – and their weekend pilots have to roar up the field with as much power under the cowling as pilot and craft can muster and take a slight left tip of the wings just after the wheels leave the ground in order to adequately clear the smoke stacks. I look down and can clearly see the insides of those stacks burning red with the trash provided by the citizens of the San Fernando Valley. I love this crazy takeoff.

We are grounded some days. Today my father scrunches along on his back with his head heading downhill inside the echoing metal skin of our little plane's fuselage. He is headed down there to adjust the ailerons. I am tasked with scouring the tarmac for stray nuts, bolts and screws. I collect these in a jar and turn them in to my father when he's done with his work. My mother takes flying lessons today so that we will always have two pilots on board as we tour the country. The first flight plan my parents decide on is to fly from California to Florida and back again. So there are many months of flying lessons for both of them and a lot of mechanical work for our plane, mostly done by my father.

At Coffin Field I can wander around under the bellies of enormous beat-up airplanes – looming, dented hulks that have livid shark's teeth painted on the nose sections. These battered craft are, of course, relics of my father's war, retired fighters from the Flying Tiger Squadron. The sides are pocked and dented and the planes squat, sinking into squashy balding tires. Alongside the shark teeth are painted figures and slogans: a side view of a naked lady with big bazooms and tiny pink lace panties along with the words "Bombs Away!" I have an intuition that these words and pictures have the same prohibitions for me as Grandma's liberal use of the word "bastards" does. I better not ask what those things mean.

I am not really clear on when or where those old planes flew or in what war. It must have been a war. The planes are snarling. At seven or eight years old, history-less, I can't picture in my imagination any time before my time and, without a visualized past, I cannot know how very close in time that I and that old war are. It will be many years later before I can identify the dates of the first atomic bombs and my own birthday, only a scant few weeks apart. Now I boast, ironically mind you, I was born two months after the first atom bombs were borne.

We were not rich; owning and maintaining a little Cessna costs much less than owning and maintaining a new Chevy back then. Snapshots show that both my mother and I wear the same pedal pushers over several years of travel. The cuffs of mine start at mid calf and end up several seasons later at my knees. And, always, my father wears his flight cap. We stay in inexpensive parking lot motels along the way – little one story house-ettes, centered on brilliant turquoise chlorine swimming pools.

The longest part is Texas. With a flight speed of around 85 miles per hour, crossing Texas takes 4 days. El Paso, Abilene, Ft. Worth, Dallas. From my jump seat behind the pilot and co-pilot, my father and mother, I clutch the earphones so that I can hear the disembodied voice of the Omni navigational system operator. As I gnaw on an apple, I listen to the hypnotic male voice, endless and endlessly calming; El Paso. 145. Om-Neee. Beeeeeep. Then electrostatic crackling and then: El Paso. 140. Om-Neee. Beeeeep. El Paso. 132. Om-Neee. Beeeeep. I love to listen to the change in destination the minute we start flying over a new zone: Abiline. 245. Om-Neee. Beeeeeeeep. Abiline. 240. Om-Neee. Beeeep.

We fly through the South—Texas, Louisiana, Mississippi. We fly at dawn to avoid the hot thermals for a few hours before landing at our next destination. Afternoons are for touring around in each town and city. We wander in public parks beneath huge trees that sag under hanging mosses. It is hot above the leaves and the gauze of the moss. We walk slowly in the thick heat. Shafts of sunlight pierce the negative spaces between the leaves and branches making patterns on the hot sidewalks. We tour city halls which display red flags with fancy "X's" slashing through them. In California our flag has a bear in the center. These red flags have a big "X" in the middle. As we wander around Mississippi and Louisiana, I see these things but I don't know what to ask about them, or whether or not I *should* ask anything about them. But I fill my vision with these images and see them still, today.

What we do in every town is to get on a bus - destination unknown to us — and we ride the whole route, all the way to the bus terminal and then, chatting with the next bus driver as he comes on duty, we ride all the way back to where we came from.

"Y'all folks don't sit back there."

The bus driver motions for us to move forward in his vehicle.

"Y'all folks sit rite t'ere back behind me, y'hear?"

I see shacks made from crooked grey wood and skinny little kids and buckets, flung empty on the ground, and ragged bony hens pecking dirt and old women in drooping flowered dresses and wood slats for stairs climb crooked porches and we sit inside our bus and the driver, fat and authoritative, motions proprietarily for us to look at this and look at that, showing us his town and the exotics who live on the periphery of his civic pride. From where I am, sitting behind him, I stare at his fat red neck as it rolls over the back of his gray bus uniform collar and I see that his neck hairs are red and sprout from his red skin, shorn and prickly. I look out the bus window and see big dusty trees. I see Nehigh Orange soda pop crates, rusted American Flyer wagons twisting in the front yards alongside broken pink dolls, headless, sprawled with their plastic limbs flung, impossible, falling, flying, floating across the red dirt yards.

I am seven or eight or nine years old during these cross country trips, an unfinished tabula rasa creature. I have no experience of people other than my people, no history or culture yet. I see and wonder about the bus antennas, each one pierced with a row of metal objects — cones and spheres and cubes. These antennae are stuck onto the outside of the front window of each bus; cone, cone, sphere, or cube, cone, sphere. The bus driver bellows over his grinding gearbox and tells us that those cones and spheres are for "them folks who cain't read". Each different combination of cones and cubes and spheres indicates a street name. Until this moment, I have seen nothing outside of my world of the San Fernando Valley's orange trees and dirt roads; nothing outside of my little neighborhood of new box tract houses and a nice little school made out of pink buildings set on fresh blacktop. So what I see, what I observe, I see here in Mississippi for the first time. But the old houses don't look so different to me from the old houses in the farming San Fernando Valley around the time when I was born. And the old ladies in flowering dresses are not shaped much differently from my own grandma back then. And in front of my grandma's house in the San Fernando Valley there had been a dirt road too. And we had hens back when I was little, pecking and scratching along grandma's dusty driveway. And I have an American Flyer red wagon, just like that one over there, except mine is shiny new.

The little kids in the Mississippi front yards stare at the bus as we roll along through their lives. Tomorrow Louisiana, four days for Texas, skip across New Mexico, sleep in Arizona, then home to Coffin Field.

When we unlock the back door to our kitchen, the house smells stuffy. It's been shut tight for two weeks, windows and doors locked. Hot and still, the afternoon sun is stifled against the yellowing shades of our living room windows. My mother snaps them up and they spin and flap around as she lifts the lower pane of each double hung window to let in the air and sunshine. My father takes off his flight cap, folding it tidy into its habitual crease and lays it down with a little pat onto the side arm of the davenport.

Benighted and Without a Bullshit Detector

Here is another story from my benighted past. Benighted being the operative word for what I was going to experience as my mother died and afterwards. Benighted: a definitive word for being overtaken by night or darkness, plunged into darkness.

About a million years ago, my father sped off to LAX for a business trip. 1968. In his haste, he forgot to pack two freshly ironed and starched dress shirts. From the airport he called me. I was home with my mother, staying there while he was gone, per my slightly altered instructions from him, about my mother's final illness. My father was going on a business trip for several days and wanted me to stay, full time, with my mother until he returned. His usual instructions to me were:

"We will take care of her. You do days. I will do nights."

But in these extenuating circumstances of his having to do a business trip, he told me to stay round the clock.

And that illness was . . .

Carcinomatosis:

From the *Oxford English Dictionary Vol. 2 p.886:*

Widespread dissemination of carcinoma throughout the body; applied also to a more limited spread when it is substantial in amount but diffuse, without the usual separate nodules.

Simple enough.

My mother's doctor, and perhaps a surgeon, performed an exploratory surgery on her abdomen after numerous tests revealed nothing detectable that could attest to her hugely swollen stomach. She looked 9 months pregnant. For her remaining days she suffered continuous nausea, and violent vomiting. Her doctor drained her abdomen several times. The exploratory surgery? Diagnosis? Widespread carcinomatosis throughout her abdomen. Very advanced. Her doctor called us after the exploratory and offhandedly quipped:

"Nine months max."

Nice guy. Comforting.

And for the following five months, she suffered, declined, and we took care of her. Me, days. My father, nights. How stupid I was. Lacking in sound judgement, I did not even notice — I was so stupid back then that I did not realize we needed a nurse. Or something. Hospice did not exist back then.

Her attacks of violent nausea and vomiting were frightening to me. So scared I was that she would die during my watch, my knees knocked as I overheard her when she was in the bathroom, door closed. I remember marveling that the phrase 'knees knocked' was an actual physical manifestation of fear. After one of her seizures, I lay down beside her on the bed and kissed her arm. Her arms, once riotously speckled with freckles, had lost them all. Not a freckle remained on what was now her pale yellow epidermis. I wondered why. She maintained some kind of modesty or protectiveness of me, or secretiveness, throughout her decline. Late in her days she asked me to shave her legs. How she could muster modesty then, I did not know. I do not know, even now. I shaved her legs and did a nice gentle tidy job while she lay back, eyes closed. Even during her last 24 hours, after we put her in an ambulance for the hospital and we followed along behind in our cars — even that evening, she got up on her own and walked briskly into the hospital bathroom.

Oh, Mama.

The very next day she went into a coma. Nobody at the hospital called to let me know. So, as usual for a normal hospital visit to her, I went to see her. Had bought her a little vase with a single blossom for a little gift but when I arrived at the hospital, I saw warning signs on the door of her room, Oxygen. No flame. And as I entered, I saw that she was plugged into oxygen and other cords, connected to a monitoring machine. I don't know. I can't remember. Just that she was lying still and making sounds as if to call out. My father was not there in that room. A Candystriper was on the other side of her bed, straightening out her covers when I arrived mid-morning of her last hours. I was alone with my mother and the Candy-striper. The girl said to me across the bedcovers:

"So, you have had a nurse?"

No.

I was so stupid. The thought had never even occurred to me.

The rest of that day is gone. I cannot remember a single moment of that afternoon. And, you must believe me, I have tried and tried to remember. I was weeping violently beside her bed. Then no memory at all. No memory follows. Not leaving her room. Not getting in my car. Not driving away. Not a single visual or visceral memory of the rest of her last day.

I cannot remember a single moment of that afternoon.

Until later that day, that evening.

We are sitting in our TV room. Just my father and I. It is early evening. The phone rings. My father listens. Says two words: "Forest Lawn." Nothing else. Hung up. Unbearable. We were both crying, sobbing, choking. He walked over to our record cabinet and, with both of his fists raised over his head, he thrashed them on the top of that cabinet with all his strength. Loud. So loud. I jumped, stopped crying. I was stunned and shocked, frightened. Shaking.

When I turned fifty, my father sent me the whole box of letters that they had written during WWII every day for the 18 months of their war-declared separation. In that box were also a handful of letters my mother wrote to her mother very near to September 30, 1968. The date she died. She was forty-six. Here is one I cling to and treasure as her assertion that I had, indeed, taken good care of her during her last months of life. That I had done my part well, when instructed. That I had been a good and loyal daughter:

"You do days. I will do nights."

20 August 1968 My mother's letter to her mother.
"They are so wonderful in caring for me.
Day after day when I had to go to my treatment one of them
would drive me there . . . they spoil me terribly . . .
They take such good care of me . . . they are like angels."

That letter was the single assurance that I had done okay. My father never said another word about those days to me. Never even a thank you. Nothing.

— • —

He was to be gone about a week or so on his business trip for the bank where he was a Vice President. He was in a big hurry to get to LAX for his flight to the out-of-town business meeting.

My mother at this point in her illness was close to dying. My father had asked me to stay with her for the whole time — both days and nights — as he would be gone nearly a week on business. When at the control panel of his Cessna, my father was always in control. Not for nothing it is called the 'control' panel. Working in the same way with his family — one kid, just me, some family — yet he sought to control me. Sometimes I have taken to call him by his own pseudonym: The Pilot. Back then, tasked with this necessary responsibility, I was too numb and afraid and blank, yet I would always be there for her during her last days. Not aware enough that we needed a nurse, I simply showed up, as instructed, and did what I was told. Only this time, the instructions included staying with her round the clock for an entire week while he was gone on business. There I stood in the hallway as she wobbled down on her way back from the bathroom where she had violent attacks of vomiting and groaning in pain. I watched her, my knees knocking, as she returned to her bed after these episodes. Her nightgown was lit from the back with the sunshine from the other bedroom window. My old bedroom down the hall, behind her. I could see her entire frame, from head to unsteady feet. If she weighed a hundred pounds it did not look it. She was a wobbling stick of her former five foot seven.

Then, all of a sudden, the phone rang and it was my father in a snit. He had left his clean starched shirts on hangers in the bedroom. Would I grab the shirts and get down to LAX quickly, quickly don't dawdle. I was never a dawdler. I jumped in my car, shirts on hangers, and sped off.

He was waiting for me on the curb in front of the LAX departure doors. He briskly grabbed the two hangered shirts, thanked me, perfunctory, and sped back inside. For his flight I suppose.

"Do not talk to your mother about her illness. Do not cry in front of her. We will take care of her."

Obedient, knowing not otherwise, I obeyed his orders. Obeyed his orders as he exercised his prerogatives in control of me. He was acting as the Pilot, engaging each and every dial on his plane's control panel. I did not make a peep. Did not contradict his orders. Did not even think, nevermind to suggest, that maybe, just maybe, we needed a nurse to help us. I did not say anything about our needing help. I did not say a word. So, herein, sadly and ironically, I demonstrate that I too was shut up by words – words that were used to control my actions. My feeble actions to take care of my mother at that desperate time were the result of orders not to talk, not to cry, but yet to take care of her. I would go downstairs to our guest bathroom and cry, silently, into our red guest towels. Then, I would go back upstairs to her bedside and I would lie down next to her on her bed after her attacks, and look into her face. And this is odd: near the very end, her face looked younger. Her features smoothed out and she looked like she was in her twenties. Yet, I had been silenced. Following my orders, I said nothing, just like Sarah, yes? And then she died.

This long-ago memory turned out to be a massive malfunction of my as yet nascent Bullshit Detector. The only functional part of that personal warning system is that I, at least, remembered the incident of the starched shirts. Puzzled over it. But never quite 'got' it.

Then nothing at all. I stayed with her for the whole week, days and nights. He returned from his business trip. And that was that.

Then suns and moons did their bit for more than thirty years. Sunrise. Sunset. three decades passed and then the incident of the ironed shirts and LAX finally came into focus for me.

Thirty years after his starched shirts and I sped to LAX to launch him on a business trip, he calls me. Wants to tell me something. Out of nowhere, it is more than thirty years past, with no context in our phone call at this moment, he says:

"I visited one of my old girlfriends in England once."

"When was that?"

"1968"

"When in 1968?"

He hurriedly got off the phone. Had to rush. Work to do. Clunk.

I went downstairs to where Gary was working on a high-technology marketing brochure for one of our clients.

"Don't let me forget this phone call."

And I told Gary all about what transpired on the phone just now. The whole weird thing. LAX. Ironed shirts. Knocking knees. Business trip. Old girlfriends. All of it. So I would not forget.

Gossip, the Noun vs. Gossip, the Verb

A week or so after my mother's funeral, The Pilot asked me if I would mind if he started to date. To see other women. And, hey, it was the Sixties. That's not such a big deal is it, I thought. Yeah. Sure. No problem. He nodded and, little had I guessed at that moment, he dove right in.

So the deal is this with silences: silences may lie within communications in words or within actions. Blank spaces of silences between utterances made aloud and utterances understood can be quite literally years. Decades. And the silence seals the words in cotton batting, a cozy metaphor for being wrapped up, contained, entrapped, for a long long time. But once the words are finally heard, really heard, the muffling of meaning is made clear. And it's as if it happened this very moment. No matter how many moments may have been hidden, a few words or a few actions: It's now clear, the meaning of those words or actions become quite shockingly clear, filled with cruel intention.

My father was always in control of his craft. The Cessna has a Control Panel for fuel consumption, altimeter, flap adjustments. Depending upon his handy-dandy Control Panel, so, too, he wanted always to be in control of me. Looking back on this part of my history, I can't resist giving my father his pseudonym: The Pilot.

Two months after the death of The Pilot's beloved co-pilot, my mother, it was Christmas. For a 'fun' holiday party, The Pilot and I invited various friends for snacks and drinks at our house. The house I had lived in from high school, through to college graduation. The Pilot's 'date' was a young woman my age. She, and future, other young 'dates' of his, would wear my dresses that I had left in the closet of my room upstairs. I saw this several times. Either in her cups, oblivious, or with intentional malice, she asked me if I knew what he had done on his numerous business trips over the years. No, I did not. Then she told me.

> *The words of this gossip were a real case of Lashon Hara. Or what I call: Lashing Horror.*

I had never known any of it. I wondered: what did his beloved co-pilot, my mother, know of any of those things?

Gossip. Again, that. When we are spoken to at a party where it is supposed to be a friendly happy gathering, we do not necessarily have our Bullshit Detectors in fullest operation. Yes, it will scan the words and the actions in the crowd, but our defenses are somewhat relaxed, especially when we are friendly with some of the guests. Especially with a gleaming glass of wine in hand. In the case of this morsel of stunning gossip, I was still so numb with grieving – this 'party' was in December of 1968 – that I was not able to put into perspective the words as they were spoken to me by this guest. Yes, it was shocking news and her language was shockingly 'dirty'. The type of language used by a woman leaning into the driver's side car window, on a back street, to a man who has pulled up to the curb and who takes in the offer, the terms, the cost. The words of this gossip were a real case of Lashon Hara. Or what I call: Lashing Horror. Her words of gossip were meant to cause harm. And the harm she selected was directed at me. And she obliterated me all right. Point blank.

A part of my world was reshaped by her words, but rather than acting on the news, I simply stopped. I did not respond. I couldn't speak. I just sat there and heard her and was paralyzed. And I said nothing in response to this gossip, the noun or her gossip, the verb. It is no small wonder that I reacted so actively observing Sarah's silence in the Akedah. I dove into creating midrash. Why had I not responded to this gossip? And why had Sarah not responded to what had nearly happened to her beloved son? Silence bound both me and Sarah. Curious. Why?

However, I never, ever, forgot her words. But I was not able to act at the moment she uttered them. I just sat there, bombarded by her gossip. I stored this memory away, saw her image seated upon one of my mother's upholstered chairs in what had been 'our' living room. And I recalled her words. Never forgot.

It was just gossip.

Wasn't it? Just?

Thirty seasons after that 'festive gathering' and the information from that guest, that *mere* gossip, my father called me and said he had visited an old girlfriend of his in England. When was that? The year he cited was shocking. 1968. That gossip long-ago affirmed exactly where he had gone when he went 'on business'. And I connected his calling me from LAX when he had forgotten his pressed shirts.

Finally.

I was finally graced with a keen sense of what was, and always had been, going on around me as I grew up. It was a gift of the gods as my nascent Bullshit Detector finally kicked in. And it has remained in good working order ever since. A perverse gift, I grant. But useful even to this day when so much of that brand of excrement is smashing into walls these days.

Now then: one problem. Now as you can see, I have equivocated around the name, the identity, of the person I refer to in his pseudonym as 'The Pilot'. Rather than a name, his is a pseudo-nicknamed character in this, my otherwise non-fictional memoir. And the gossip at the party — she doesn't even merit a pseudonym. Yet, I shall remain discretely behind that pseudonym and I can assure any and all of my step-relatives of my father's later life that they were not there at that benighted Christmas party. Nor were they even yet dreamed of when I delivered the starched shirts to LAX. I was there. They were not.

Recollection of that long-ago gossip — the verb and the noun — was deeply hurtful. It took place in my own mother's living room, on one of her favorite chairs, and the gossip-er? Was she wearing one of my own dresses? Twice I saw this — two of my dresses worn by two of his girlfriends. These were dresses I had left in my old bedroom's closet, worn by two of his girl-friends, so-called. The gossip's words were hushed, but nonetheless venomous. The content and thrust of her gossip were surrounded by the environment, our living room through part of high school and all of college for me. During that gossip episode, enacted in that living room, in what had been my home brought that familiar safe living room crashing down around me. My home, that familiar upholstered room drastically shifted. It wobbled and swerved and blew into smithereens. That gossip and the source of that gossip, the gossip herself, utterly destroyed that living room for me. Gossip. Powerful words that can injure and obliterate. In the moments of her gossip I realized how utterly benighted I had been throughout my previous extant life, cosseted within my little family. In the dark, deliberately so? Probably. And so, I discovered, roughly, suddenly, shockingly how ignorant of my 'real' life I had been. How delusional I had been. And so I could add ignorance to the darkness that had surrounded my family life before 1968 of my mother's death. Yet, let me assure you, dear reader, this gossip — the woman who spewed her gossip at me on that day — she did not later become a member of my family bloodline. After her barrage that day, she disappeared, utterly, from my life.

There is yet another aspect to understanding spoken words — that of a requirement that we remember and then understand and feel that certain words may be linked to forgiveness? Or, conversely, linked to NOT forgiving past words? In effect there may be lifetime silences, tamped down spoken words, inside all of us, but subject to future consideration and perhaps future actions. This is a variety of domestic silence. Everyday pauses in words spoken and actions taken. With the possibility of very great amounts of time between the spoken words and the actions taken. Is this possible? Well, there may be masses of old words remembered and reactions to those old words. Think of family squabbles at Thanksgiving tables. Think of that thing your mother or your sister or your former or present spouse — that horrible thing they said and you NEVER forget it. It comes up again and again in future arguments.

You always said . . .

Remember when you told me . . . You're impossible!

We've most of us experienced such recurring memories of words spoken and remembered for the rest of our lives. And many times, we suppress our own memories of certain actionable spoken words just to keep peace in the family.

There is yet another aspect of how on Earth we talk and that is the current bugaboo called 'freedom of speech'. It's more and more in our daily news. For the sake of brevity, I will only say this: look it up. Key it in and you will receive literally hundreds, maybe thousands, of definitions and examples of legal or illegal or constitutional or unconstitutional case histories. It's the topic du jour lately. I need to let this subject drift. Freedom of Speech. Go away. Maybe for another time. Another book. More and more and more words and words about spoken words labeled 'freedom of speech'. They're out there. But later, later I say.

N'est ce pas?

During spoken French, there are numerous tiny hissing utterances that seek to affirm what was just said. So, I heard many 'n'est ce pas' phrases scattered throughout even the simplest verbal exchanges in French. It means: 'isn't it?' A nice clipped negative phrase. Interestingly, French has several negative phrases for English phrases. For example: 'nature morte' for museum paintings that we would label: 'still life'. This may have something to do with how we interpret the word 'gossip'.

When I spoke just now about gossip, the speaker and the spoken, I told how a particular relic of long-ago gossip demolished me. Certainly, it destroyed any preconceived notions I may have had when I heard the gossip. How it made me go blank. To black out. And it would take me years to come to terms with that hurtful episode of gossip. It was vicious. N'est ce pas? Isn't it? Wasn't it?

Okay, let's delve even a bit deeper into this cruel gossip.

First: why on earth would this woman tell me this? Why? I don't get it. To serve what purpose? To ingratiate herself with me? That's crazy. To ingratiate herself with someone else, namely the host of this crummy holiday celebration? Well how does that work? Yeah, put the girl, me, in her place? Like that? Is that it? Sitting here in my own mother's upholstered living room, me, this overprotected, cosseted, privileged rich girl? Make her step back a pace from her privilege, right? To put me in my place? Show the old boy that, yes, he was right to blame me for all his failures. Was that it? Well, at least I can assure you readers of one thing for certain: this young thing did not marry into my family, what was left of it. She utterly disappeared from my life immediately after her duties as gossip. I never saw her again.

Yet. Yet. I am made anxious by writing down this incident, putting it into black and white. With today's current fad of litigation for many forms of speaking, am I likely to get one of those letters? Blaming me for causing hurt to this gossip? Or upon the subject of her gossip?

I realize now that there is even more to this discovering how on Earth we speak: credibility. How do we evaluate spoken words after the fact of speaking? How do we credit some words as truthful and how do we discredit other words as in-credible. And, perversely, naggingly, how might my own credibility come into question as I relate this gossip and it's long-lasting effects on me? How my tongue was bound for years in fear of speaking aloud of it. Yes, then we move along to how the mind, mine and perhaps every single person who opens their mouth to speak. How does the mind perceive – perception being the activating word for how on Earth we speak.

Being neither a philosopher nor psychologist, I have to wonder how on Earth we process spoken words within the convoluted cervices of our brains. How on earth can, or may, human beings process the spoken words of others when we are so jam-packed and crammed with years and decades and lifetimes of events and of conversations and of conclusions drawn and conclusions, either positive or negative, are then held to be truths? How can I, for a tiny example of human frailty, how can I draw the conclusion that that gossip – both the speaker of such and the subject of her words – how can I conclude that she was correct? That she told the truth though it was filthy gossip. Why could I not have concluded that she had been merely deluded or perhaps mentally unfit? How come I gave such instantaneous validity to her words? How come I froze in that instant and in that room? How come I kept her gossip as painful and secret? Why am I so plagued with nightmares because, here and now, these decades later, I am freeing my frozen speech? Why now? To what purpose?

You see, I am circling around my initial question: How on Earth do we Speak?

Let me be precise: this young woman with what I received

with her supposed, in my mind, wicked intention never became a part of my bloodline. NEVER. She vanished from my life. She was gone after her barrage of words.

This gossip, the person, utterly disappeared from my future life.

Shrug. Just get over it Mary. Shrug? Is that it?

There is something here about perception that now needs attention as I ponder How on Earth we speak. It's similar to the concept that each time we review the *Torah* portion during our year of study, we come to it as a different person with different perceptions about what words, mere words, may mean or may contain during this, the umpteenth time we read those words. I eventually came to view Sarah's part in *Torah* as adumbrated, if not intentionally removed. Lost? Edited out? Not certain. But I saw and heard, for perhaps the first time in my study of her story, I saw that Sarah was not present. Not in narration. Not in recorded speech. Not a word from or about Sarah in the Akedah. Surely this related to my own silences. Yes? And, as if poked by a sharp stick in delayed recognition, I saw that as Sarah's tongue was bound, so, too, had been mine.

N'est ce pas?

Yet, Silence Too May Speak Out

What if that's true? That there is substantial evidence in *Torah* for important meaning handed to us by silences? Let's turn again to Genesis 22:1-19 and Genesis 23:

> *"GENESIS CHAPTER 22: And it happened after these things that God tested Abraham. And He said to him, "Abraham!" and he said, "Here I am." And He said, "Take, pray, your son, your only one, whom you love, Isaac, and go forth to the land of Moriah and offer him up as a burnt offering on one of the mountains which I shall say to you." And Abraham rose early in the morning and saddled his donkey and took his two lads with him, and Isaac his son, and the split wood for the offering, and rose and went to the place that God had said to him. . . . Abraham took the wood for the offering and put it on Isaac his son and he took in his hand the fire and the cleaver, and the two of them went together. And Isaac said to Abraham his father, "Father! And he said,*
>
> *"Here I am, my son."*
>
> *And he said "here is the fire and the wood but where is the sheep for the offering?"*

> *And Abraham said, "God will see to the sheep for the offering, my son." . . .*
> *CHAPTER 23: And Sarah's life was a hundred and twenty-seven years, the years of Sarah's life."*

So that was it? Not a word from Sarah? Not a written sentence in those chapters that supposedly tell her story? There is NO THING recorded in our most sacred Jewish document, about or from, the words about or from Sarah, most beloved, and revered, of our matriarchs?

If I were to read it as I had not read it before, this is what I might see. I now apprehend Sara's silences in a way I had not understood or grasped before — that Sarah says no thing in these chapters. But, now, today, I find something else. That there is not a single peep from the narration from her lips. Yes, that is so. So now, how on earth could I glean something positive and valuable from those absent words. What if I could, instead, squeeze out positive information about, say, how on Earth we may speak with silences?

Let's give this a test.

Here is yet another memory I still carry into 2025. Clearly I recall and now see this silent communication here in my 80th year.

I am invited to a wedding. The ceremony is to be conducted in the living room of a house with a minister standing on the hearth. In this living room are seated guests on little white squeaky folding chairs. Rented. I see that all the chairs are occupied. I step up to the front row to find my seat held for me. But no. That front row center chair is occupied and I am glared away. Not here for you, Mary Carter. Not for you, Mary.

I shuffle around the living room and there are no empty seats. I find my way to the rear of the living room, back into the entry hall and push my way next to the front door of the house. From there I cannot see the minister at the hearth. I am standing among assorted neighbors and their spouses, the gardener in a suit, barely recognizable without his tan canvas hunting helmet. The bride swishes down the stairs, swings past me, winks. I am shoulder to shoulder with our next door neighbor, a good friend of my mother. We can hear the words begin and I have tears. Silent, unobtrusive. The neighbor lady, tactful, also unobtrusive, slides her arm around my waist, draws me firm to her side. She holds me throughout the ceremony. Then the ceremony is complete. The neighbor, carefully and discreetly withdraws her supporting arm, her support of and her acknowledgement of my anguish. She has said in silence, 'I see how you feel. I can do this small thing to give you

So silence, as we see in Genesis, may communicate to us — students of Torah in 2025, that silence, too, may be part of how on Earth we speak.

silent support.'

I have never forgotten her support. I know it now as I did back then, and I heard what she said to me, in silence.

And so, as silent and as absent as Sarah in Genesis, this neighbor's support communicated – spoke to me – in silence.

My Delayed Response to Vietnam 1995

I have another notable delayed response in my repertoire of reactions to spoken words. During the era of the Vietnam War, I was a teenager and then later I turned twenty-one. But, other than the occasional Vietnam vet, I did not have any contemporaneous boyfriends who were drafted or served back then. And so, I rode along in the optimistic fluorescent sixties, listening to Bob Dylan and the Jefferson Airplane. Go ask Alice. Who was I back then? Not even a shadow of myself had fully emerged at that time. But the sound track was good, WOW. Fersure!

At some point around December of 1967 I got a little hand-written note from the roommate that had been my boyfriend, so-called, that Marc had died. Likely by his own hand. Likely in his own Cessna. That's all. Had he been drafted? In despair? Desperate? The thought never occurred to me back then. Wrapped up in my pink bunting, I never gave him a thought about why or how come, he died. Amazing. How dim and self-centered I was back then. I was not really living in that Vietnam era. Oblivious. Stupid. I vaguely, yes, did repeat to myself:

"What are we going to do now, Mary Carter."

Very likely Marc's last words to me.

So the fact, the non-fiction, of Marc's death got all wound about in the tangle of my own flawed and vacuous perception of the facts of those times. I experienced Vietnam very much after the fact. Vietnam came later, much later, into my life. It would be 1995 when it came home to me. And then, even later, when I wrote about it in my monograph *A Death Delayed Agent Orange: Hidden Killer of Vietnam.*

So let's remember that dinner guest who asked me:

"Ah so. Do you write about yourself in all your books?"

Let's test that question and see if that dinner guest's question has merit. What follows is an event from my own life that I wrote about. What follows are excerpts from this book, published in 2017. Used with permission of me, myself.

A Death Delayed

Agent Orange:

Hidden Killer of Vietnam

A Remembrance

By Mary E. Carter

Excerpt 1995:

It is estimated that between 1962 and 1971, almost 11 million gallons of Agent Orange [a powerful herbicide] were sprayed in Vietnam, primarily through an aerial spray program code-named Operation Ranch Hand."

What is presumptive service-connected Agent Orange disability compensation?

Scientific evidence has demonstrated that there is an association between development of certain disabling medical conditions and exposure to Agent Orange and other related herbicides [if] the veteran served in the Republic of Vietnam, regardless of the length of that service, during the period January 9, 1962 and May 7, 1975.

I sit in the darkened room with the dying man. I do not know this man, having only met him three days ago. I am here with his fiancée, Elizabeth, to keep her company while she visits with him, Danny, during his last few days. He is dying from wounds sustained in Vietnam.

Danny's room, this hospital room, faces west and the

sun has just set, garish purple and red, and dusk now dimly illuminates a fiery red maple tree across the street from us; the only one on the block still in leaf. Elizabeth and I are here in this hospital room along with two of Danny's oldest friends, Willy and his wife, Louise. Looking away, I look out the window, now black and reflecting us back to ourselves. The light from the hospital hallway wedges in across the foot of the hospital bed and we hear loud talk and crashing and gurgling aspirators. Someone jauntily throws a used syringe into the wastebasket across the hall which is marked, hasty and spelled wrong: 'Medical waste. No recycl'. It's 1995.

Danny sits high on his bed with the top cranked up. His eyes are closed and he moves his head slightly as if he were watching a movie from too close. His mouth is open and he moves it very subtly in gestures as if he were speaking to a companion. We see that he has two Tic Tacs on the end of his tongue. He holds his hands still, facing upwards, arms crooked at the elbows in a seeming pantomime of holding something. We watch him. Then we look away. Suddenly Danny bursts out, shouting:

"You trust that guy?"

We jump, startled.

He shouts again:

"You trust that guy?"

Belligerent, he faces me:

"Huh? Huh? You trust that guy?"

He moves his arms into a weapon-pointing gesture, aiming with his eyes closed, he nudges his hallucination and shoves it along with the barrel of his imaginary weapon. Then, as suddenly as he began, he stops, arms lowering, silent. He is quiet now.

The VA recognizes more than 50 illnesses and diseases connected to Agent Orange exposure. Most of these are cancers. They can occur at any time after service in Vietnam, including decades after exposure. Enemies were hidden everywhere in the jungles of Vietnam and, as it turns out, another form of enemy could hide within the very cells of the soldiers who served there.

This is the last battlefield — a thin high bed with a plastic mattress cover and soft, wrinkled, limp, over-laundered sheets. This soldier sits on a rumpled little plastic pad which is wired like an electric blanket, I suppose. When he gets up and tries to leave the bed, a buzzer sounds and one of us leaps over to flip a little switch to turn off the intrusive warning. He is up. He is agitated. Help him. The last uniform is a cotton nightie, tied in the back to expose to his enemies his delicate wing bones. The last weapon is morphia.

Later that evening, Elizabeth and I sit in a Mexican restaurant. Picking at her cheese enchilada, she sighs:

"He was in Vietnam today."

"Yes. I think so" . . .

"Hey, Buddy!"

Friend for life, a kid from the neighborhood. Danny's buddy, Willy, always calls him 'Buddy'. Willy is all heat and energy and muss as he charges up to the bedside and kisses Danny on the cheek. Danny's head pops up and sideways and he says in a weak thin voice:

"Hey Willy! Not bad. Not bad. Good, in fact. Sure."

Willy slides out of his down coat and tosses it at the radiator. It skis down onto the floor.

"Well, Jack's coming today, Buddy. Finally."

He glances at me and Elizabeth.

"You hear about that, Danny? Did he call you?"

"Oh, hey. No. Nobody told me. Good. That's good. Oh, hey, wait. Yeah. Somebody did tell me. You told me already, didn't you?"

Danny frowns and blinks and looks up at Willy. Willy mocks:

"Yeah, Buddy. I never tell you nothing. Is that what you're sayin'?"

Abruptly, Danny hoists himself up, bending his knees, doing a skinny sit up and reaching shakily for his feet. He bobs back and forth, back and forth, rocking and holding his toes, his knees bent to his chest. Willy pulls a chair to the head of the bed, turns it facing into the bed, looks around the room, at the blinds, at the bedside table, at us, then back to Danny. Danny is frowning and his forehead puckers and his eyes look frantic. He rocks back and forth, back and forth. Then, suddenly so that we all jump a little, he spins on his butt and he's sitting sidesaddle on the edge of the hospital bed and he swings his yellowish skinny legs back and forth, back and forth, and bobs his trunk up and down. He shouts:

"Madre!"

Willy, still and quiet and big and plain, looks, steady, at him for a moment:

"You want to go to the john?"

Danny bobs up and down, looking sideways at Willy.

"Yeah, man. You mind?"

Willy stands as Danny slides off the bed onto his stocking feet. Danny bends slightly forward from the waist and gestures, shaky and frowning, waving his fingers to grasp Willy's arm. Willy guides him to the bathroom, closes the door and as the door swings shut we see Willy holding Danny strong and easing him onto the toilet.

Elizabeth looks at me. Her eyes brim with tears for a second, then they are gone. We both turn to look out the window. Willy steps back into the room and closes the door behind him:

"He'll be in there for a while."

We hear Danny moaning in there.

Danny served in Vietnam in 1968. He was a Long-Range Reconnaissance Patrolman. A LRRP. In 1968 Martin Luther King, Jr. was assassinated. Robert Kennedy was assassinated. The Tet Offensive begins. The Tet Offensive ends. McNamara resigns. President Johnson says he won't run again. Stock market soars. Riots. Les événements in Paris. Nixon is elected President. Agent Orange sprayed liberally in Vietnam. Your average lousy year.

Now it's 1995.

This afternoon, Danny moves constantly. He moves with great loud bursts of physicality, sudden gestures and grunts. You would not think he had the strength at this point to move so much and so frequently and so rapidly, scooting up and down the bed, whirling from one side to another with surprising fiendish dexterity, shouting:

"Ey, yi, yi, yi, yi."

Then shifting to flail arms and legs, moaning, he shouts:

"Madre!"

Willy studies him during these moments.

"You in pain, Buddy?"

"Not particularly," Danny answers.

Then he amends:

"Yes. Yes. Yes. I am. I think."

"Where does it hurt, Buddy?"

Willy looks at him sideways and blank, the only thing on his great quiet face that moves is his nostrils.

"Well. I hurt here." Danny places a hand on his stomach.

"And here." He touches the back of his head.

"And here, I think." He moves his hand to the top of his head.

"I don't know. It's hard to say. It's all just one big thing."

He bobs his head over in Willy's direction, petulantly; he's like a child with the flu:

"I don't know. I don't know! Why're you asking me?"

Then Danny starts bobbing, back and forth, back and forth, eyes squinting tight, frowning, mouth open. His feet are jutting around under the sheet.

Willy looks at me and Elizabeth and says, softly:

"I think it's time."

And he gets up and strides out to the nurse's station.

Big, warm, chip on his shoulder, Willy. Unlikely angel

flying into the hospital room in his huge, rustling nylon down jacket. Cocky, talking talk, walking like it's lunch-time at the factory. Wide and beer gut and so what's it to YOU?

I imagine, because I did not see, rather I intuited, that Willy gets home from the hospital some days and sits on the bed next to his wife, his pretty high school sweetheart. Willy sits snug in next to her. He's in his shorts, knees splayed, crying big snuffling sobs and wet tears because Buddy is dying.

"I calls him that since we was kids. Bud. Or Buddy. Or Butthead."

He sniffles, loud:

"After Nam, I guess was when we started kissing each other. You know. It's just friends. Nothing else. We been through all that. And now this."

And, because of 'this', Willy quits his job a few months back. Drives Danny to all his appointments; doctors, tests, procedures, treatments. Helping Danny's mother. Whatever needs doing, Willy's there and it's done. It's what you do.

Here's your brochure, issued in 1995 by the Vietnam Veterans of America, Inc. This little brochure is commendable for its terse simplicity. In just 18 pages the authors sum up the use of, exposure to, scope of, litigation pending, and benefits for cancers synonymous with exposure to Agent Orange in Vietnam.

"The VA presumes exposure to Agent Orange for veterans who served in Vietnam."

This brochure lists diseases and conditions eligible for disability and death benefits. The second one is Non-Hodgkin's Lymphoma (NHL). Danny's disease.

Below that, the reader learns that,

"To win disability compensation or death benefits for Non-Hodgkin's Lymphoma (NHL) a veteran or survivor must show that the veteran served in Vietnam and he or she developed NHL at any time after service. No proof of exposure to Agent Orange is necessary."

This is followed by two brief summaries of litigation:

Nehmer (VVA) v. Veterans Administration: a win for veteran's benefits. And a class action suit against the manufacturers of Agent Orange called: Agent Orange Product Liability Litigation, MDL No. 381. It's another win for veterans with a multi-million-dollar Settlement Fund, dated December 31, 1994.

Imagine.

A war with a 25-year fuse. People hit by something, wounded, dying as surely as if they had stopped a bullet in, say, 1968, but not dying immediately. Dying, instead, at age 47 or 51. Thought they were lucky to come back alive in '68.

Magnanimously, the VA presumes exposure to Agent Orange by every 'body' that served in Vietnam. Not that it's all that easy to collect your benefits. Just try getting your application through. Gotta be sick a year from your application date. Problem is: you can be dead by then. So, you maybe receive your benefits just in time for the first anniversary of your disease and you're so sick you cannot even understand that you are sick.

If your best buddy, Willy, tells you that you got your benefits and you can hear him and understand him through brain tumors and chemo therapy and if you're not in too much pain today and if you can remember what Willy said five minutes ago:

"Hey Buddy. You got your benefits."

What Is Agent Orange?

We learn in the pages of the VA brochure,

"Agent Orange is an herbicide made from a combination of two compounds: 2,4-D and 2,4,5-T, technically known as chlorinated phenoxy acids. The most dangerous element of Agent Orange is a contaminant present in the manufacture of 2,4,5-T; this impurity is known chemically as 2,3,7,8-tetrachlorodibenzo-paradioxin or, more commonly, dioxin."

Farther down the page it reads:

"Agent Orange, so named because it was shipped in 55 gallon drums marked with orange stripes. In Vietnam, herbicides were sprayed from fixed and rotary wing aircraft, trucks and backpack sprayers to clear vegetation around fire bases, landing zones, and along river banks."

And get this:

"It is estimated that between 1962 and 1971, almost 11 million gallons of Agent Orange were sprayed in Vietnam, primarily through an aerial spray program code-named Operation Ranch Hand."

Danny is dying from Non-Hodgkin's Lymphoma. He has tumors in his groin, abdomen, and brain. And if that won't kill you, modern medicine will. His waxy skin has a pale-yellow translucence and stretches across his back and cranium, taut. His bald head has two scars which now seal up the direct access routes which were used for the deadly healing chemicals of conventional cancer therapy. His chest is pierced with a utilitarian little shunt which is used to expedite other chemicals into veins in his chest. But you know what? He's growing a beard. White and bristling. It even needs a trim right now. Yet he's bald as a gnome. Then, as if the bloody urine, loss of appetite, the enormous and swelling tumor in his neck, the aphasia — as if all that were not enough, he sprouts bed sores, overnight, which are plastered over with a peculiar plastic adhesive 'skin' which very gentle nurses apply as they talk and joke with him.

Agent Orange is ". . . an herbicide made from a combination of two compounds."

Suddenly Willy asks us, "Well, I say it's the nuns. You okay with that, Elizabeth?"

Hospice. This is where the last great battles of nations are fought. Futile battles. Stupid skirmishes. This is the meeting place for a hopeless and perverse truce between good and evil. It is the place where nuns do good work to provide 'last aid' for soldiers who are dying from the evil of warfare.

Danny lies here in this place, dying as surely from his wounds as if he had stopped a bullet in Vietnam in 1968. Of the many enemies hidden in those jungles, Agent Orange was perhaps the most insidious. It hid within the very bodies of soldiers who returned home from those jungles without apparent wounds. You might as well have ordered his body bag in '68. Kept it in a trunk.

On our last evening with Danny, his mother arrives. She is immaculately dressed, a tiny woman in a knit suit.

She sits on a chair, spine upright, hands around her purse, silent, just looking at her son. We see her this one last evening, silhouetted in the window with the glare of the setting sun outside.

I cannot imagine how Elizabeth summoned the strength to leave Danny the following morning. It was her last moment to embrace her lover. I stepped out into the hallway and closed the door. I could hear nothing from behind that closed door. After a time, maybe twenty minutes, maybe a little more, she appeared suddenly in the hallway. Walking quickly, forcefully, she said to me:

"Let's go. Now."

I had been anxious about this last day for Elizabeth with Danny, but it turned out to be eerily silent. I had worried that Elizabeth would leave Danny's room sobbing or screaming or that she would collapse by his bedside in retching grief. So, I was surprised by her appearance of self-possession as she opened the door and rapidly rejoined me the hallway. No tears. No sobs. She was calm. Her face was blank and pale. Her eyes were wide and dry. Perhaps her calmness was, rather, numbness. I do not know.

We fumbled around on the polished linoleum, helping each other into our coats, scarves, gloves. God knows how she was able to walk down that hallway and to leave the building on that last day, knowing she would never see him again. Elizabeth walked, long strides, whisking down the polished linoleum, moving fast out ahead of me. Her rain coat made wings as she flew along, through the lobby, faster, faster, out the doors and into the drizzle. One of the neighborhood friends was holding open the car doors. We got in quickly. Slammed the doors. He drove off, fast. Off we went, off to the airport for the long flight home.

A few days later, back home, Elizabeth called me in the evening. She was sobbing. She could barely form words as she gasped and choked.

"It's so unfair. It's just so unfair."

Now Danny was gone forever. And now Elizabeth could allow the collapse of that deep fissure in her reserves. Sobbing and rambling she told me that she had wanted to keep herself together for him. To not upset him with her grief. To be there, beautiful as she had always been, for him. And through bitter tears, she just kept sobbing:

"It's just not fair. It's so unfair."

And after all these years I realize that this, too, is where the last great battles of nations are fought; deep within the broken hearts of those who are left behind. There is nothing left to do except to continue to live, alone, after the deaths of the soldiers. Those broken hearts; yet more casualties of the hidden killers of Vietnam."

I wrote this essay in 1995 as a memento for my friend who was devastated by the loss of her fiancée. I gave it to her, then put the manuscript on a shelf where it resided until 2017. Cleaning out a closet, I rediscovered it.

This really happened. For privacy, I have changed the names of the people in this soldier's story.

Brave Girl or Foolish?

So I suppose you may remember how I got rid of a man with a gun in our synagogue parking lot? I mean, I've told this story a million times haven't I? But, talk about things still being on our minds, this thing really sticks in mine.

So, Okay. Okay. Here goes:

It starts simple.

Once upon a time there was man with a gun over there.

On a Friday, January 20th in 2017, I steered my car into our synagogue parking lot. I was a few minutes early for a *Torah* Study class that I had been attending for several seasons.

Another car pulled into the space next to my driver's side. That would have been nothing unusual as our class included about a half dozen regulars. Also, we shared our Friday venue at the synagogue with another, secular, group. Other cars would soon be coming into the parking lot for both gatherings.

Glancing to my left, I watched as the driver of the car next to me got out of his car. He opened the rear door of his car, on the driver's side of his vehicle, and started to buckle up a large belt around his waist. Then he reached into the back seat and picked up a handgun. I saw the weapon as he slid it into his holster. It was a man with a gun over there.

Without hesitation, I got out of my car and strode right up to him using a certain tone, an ornery shout, and I yelled right into his face:

"HEY! WHAT ARE YOU DOING?"

Then I kept yelling:

"You can't do that here! This is a synagogue!"

He started chattering — scattered, nervous — telling me something not very coherent about being in our parking lot to rendezvous with some other officers for something that I couldn't quite make out. I asked for his identification. He handed me a very beat up wallet with a beat up looking piece of printed matter and a battered badge that I did not recognize as any kind of badge I had ever seen before. I handed the wallet back to him and said,

I was not afraid. I acted.

"This doesn't mean anything to me!"

Then he asked if I minded if he loaded another weapon. Unbelievable! And I shouted again:

"YOU CANT DO THAT HERE. THIS IS A SYNAGOGUE."

He asked if I minded if he parked along the street, at the curb directly in front of our parking lot. I cannot remember exactly what I said — something to the effect of 'suit yourself'. As he pulled his car around, I walked behind it and jotted down the car's license plate number.

Then he parked his car over onto the side street right next to our synagogue parking lot.

At that point my other study partners started arriving. I told them about the man. He was now in his car, parked directly adjacent to our parking lot, on the street, about twenty feet away from us. We decided to immediately leave the premises. We knew that the building was locked because the administrator had locked up and was doing errands off-site. One of our group informed the other study group members about the situation and they left too. Our group drove up the street to a restaurant where I called 911 and reported the 'a man with a gun over there'.

No police ever showed up to our synagogue to check things out.

Now here's the thing:

I simply got out of my car and approached a man with a gun. I did not rationalize. I was not afraid. I acted.

The absence of fear in my autonomic nervous system at that moment demonstrated to me, exactly how much beyond rationality, how beyond fear, my action must be. And how beyond skin deep, my mikvah had taken me. And thus, the embodiment of something quite unsuspected had embraced my Jewish self: fearlessness. I was not afraid.

Of course, I had already embraced my Jewish life — in

study, in observances, the annual recital of the Al Chet, a new me under the Huppah, my new name at the mikvah. And in what I sometimes call bashert, the *Torah* portion on the day of my birth was *Lech L'echa:*

> *"Go from your land, from your birthplace and from your father's house, to the land which I will show you."*

And now, with a man right over there, a man with a gun, my Jewish life was about to confront me with its needs. Now the test. I aimed my Jewish self, point blank, at a man with a gun and I yelled:

"WHAT ARE YOU DOING?"

I discovered that my Jewish embodiment combined conscious thought with reflexes, with instinct, brain with muscle. My Jewish mind was about to become reflexive rather than merely reflective. I got out of my car. I walked right up to a man with a gun. I hollered at him.

It was later, much later, that I thought about what I had done.

Not for a moment had I been afraid. Not at that moment. And not ever since. And not now. Not today as I tell my story here. In fact, I am not even afraid of telling this story yet again to all of you. I'm not afraid of boring you telling it yet again. I am fearless. Right?

Afterwards, my friends from *Torah* class, bless each and every one of them, they yelled at me:

"Don't ever do that again!"

I cannot honestly say I would never do that again. Any more than I cannot slam on the brakes if a dog runs in front of my car. Any more than a Mama Lion cannot lash out at a threat to her kittens. No. I can't promise I would not do that again.

There was a man. Over there. With a gun. That was that.

Later, another friend called me. She had a dear friend who was, at that moment, dying slowly of a debilitating stroke. My friend had been sitting by her friend's bedside for several days. My friend said to me:

"You know, what you did in the parking lot — there are worse ways to die."

I acknowledge that, yes, that's true. There are many long slow painful declines which result in the death of the body, the mind, the soul.

Now there is just onc more element to my telling you about the man with a gun. And it is this: I decided to write an article for one of the Jewish publications. Something along the line of instincts blooming after *Torah* study, after my mikvah.

Then another friend warned me that writing and publishing something about the man with the gun could serve to lure out the crazies and might put our congregation on the target of an antisemitic nut-case who might want to reenact what I have described here, or worse, God forbid, to actually shoot someone. My friend is afraid of repercussions if I tell anyone about my experience.

And so I delete the name of my congregation from this essay.

I delete my city.

I delete my state.

My friend warns me that she is afraid. And this creates in me a fear of my own.

I try to obliterate this fear – not of the man with the gun. But of my fear of hurting my friend.

And so I delete my name from this essay.

And so I delete my ‘self’ from this essay.

And so I censor my ‘self’.

And so then?

Then what?

I write *nothing* about my experience?

Censored by somebody else’s fear of repercussions?

And I say nothing?

But I was not afraid when I approached the man with the gun. Not in the moment of my reflexive action. Nor later.

And yet, too, I understand how fear works on a body.

Yet, now I was embodied – heart, mind, soul, right into the marrow of my bones. But, if I censor myself, then who will I be?

So now, when one of my friends speaks to me carefully about her fears of 'repercussions' if I write about the man with the gun, would it truly be my fault if there were to be any repercussions to my telling my story? I wrestle with my responsibilities – my own and my responsibilities to my friends, and of course, to my own, now fearless, Jewish self.

So, now, I am warned that if I write about my experience there could be repercussions. Now I needed to beware of both the effect of the man with the gun and also beware of inciting the worst fears of my friends.

Beware of what?

Of getting shot?

Beware of repercussions?

Beware of bullets?

Beware of words?

Beware of copycats?

Of bullets?

Of blood?

Of words? Mere words?

But I ask: wouldn't I, conversely, dis-embody myself by *not* talking about it?

Disembodied, I am less myself.

Disembodied, I'm a ghost.

Or numb.

Victimized.

Or dead.

There's no winning this one. Gun or no gun, I could be disembodied either way. Disembodied by his gun. Or disembodied by my own silence if I am too afraid to talk or write about the man with a gun over there.

But you've read this far. Where should I come out on this?

See what I mean? I am still wrestling with that man and his gun.

And get this:

These days synagogues in my state are having meetings with FBI and local police forces and bring in professional guard organizations, to protect our grounds and parking lots during classes and services. Now we have guards around our synagogue parking lots to protect us from men with guns.

Ironic, isn't it. Guards with guns in my synagogue parking lot. No need for me to step up now. Right?

I had already passed my trial by fire when I fired off my mouth with:

"HEY! WHAT ARE YOU DOING?"

I yelled at that man with his gun. All those years ago.

Next time I meet a man with a gun, or hear words of antisemitism for example, I have words. I am stronger now. And I will not shut up. It doesn't work that way.

Years ago, I shouted at that man with his gun in our synagogue parking lot:

"HEY! WHAT ARE YOU DOING?"

And I shall shout, again and again, to the all the men with their guns and to hatred and to enormous antisemitic crowds all over the globe I will shout, as many times as it takes:

"HEY! WHAT ARE YOU DOING?"

Which Brings Me to My Mikvah
Excerpts from
A Non-Swimmer Considers Her Mikvah

For this section I take quotes from my book *A Non-Swimmer Considers Her Mikvah.* It was the first book I wrote using my new Jewish voice. A memoir of how I became Jewish after age fifty. Four other books with Jewish themes would follow. All novels. Each book was judged WINNER in the New Mexico-Arizona Book Awards, Religion Category.

Here is an excerpt from *A Non-Swimmer Considers Her Mikvah:*

> ### *Lech L'cha! Get Going!*
>
> *As a teenager I fainted at every movie theater in Los Angeles — the Wiltern, the Paramount, the Chinese and the Egyptian. Waiting in line for Ben Hur, for Gone with the Wind, for The Pink Panther, for Lawrence of Arabia, I fainted.*
>
> *My mother was an elementary school teacher so she and I shared all the school holidays. Summer was for the movies. Standing in line with my mother, on our long hot summer vacations in L.A., I would first feel a wave of*

panic, a woozy feeling in my belly and a ringing in my ears. Then a hot flush started in my body like a wave at the beach lapping up my legs and arms and I knew I would have to sit down or that I would drop down. Not wanting to disappoint my mother, and, really, really wanting to see the movie, I would try to wait it out, breathing in, breathing out. In. And out. In. Out. But it never got better. My vision would darken around my eyebrows as sparkling spots of darkness circled in my eyes. Then cottony deafness and voices receded. Softly, slowly, I would float into what sounded like a bed of cornflakes. I was never injured, protected by the oblivious looseness of my limbs in my fainting free-fall.

Then suddenly, surprisingly, and very loud, I would hear my mother's alarmed voice near my ear,

"Mary. Mary!"

Then she would get mad.

"You're not eating properly!"

And I would protest,

"But Mama . . ."

She would push aside the other moviegoers in line and rush me into the theater lobby for a Snickers. Then we'd sit in the cold lobby, side by side on old red velvet couches, bare summer sleeveless arms touching, breathing in the buttery smell of popcorn. We sat there recuperating, me wobbly and picking at my candy medicine. Then she'd start.

She'd regale me with one of her longish speeches about proper nutrition, about always starting the day with a good breakfast, about vitamins and especially about the lack of enough calcium in my diet. And then she'd change tack ever so gracefully and observe how hot it was, really too hot, anyone could have fainted in that heat and how the box office had not opened on time so we'd had to stand there too long and how it's no wonder that I had fainted. And suddenly she was on my side, defending me against all reason because that's how she was. Quickly her mind turned around. That's how she never found fault with me, but with circumstances. And with me still nibbling my candy bar, but starting to perk up, we'd decide that, yes, I felt better and let's go in and find a nice cool seat and enjoy the movie. Which we inevitably did.

The landmarks of my childhood: the Wiltern, the Paramount, the Chinese and the Egyptian. Not the Hollywood sign perched and crooked up on that historic hillside. Not the iconic palm trees along the California streets, but places where I had fainted. Those were my landmarks.

I introduce them here to demonstrate and to personalize Parsha Lech L'cha, Genesis 12, which is what we are studying this month.

It contains God's instructions to Abraham:

"Go forth from your land, your birthplace, your father's house,to the land I will show you."

It can be wrenching to leave your birthplace, your land, your father's house, literally, to leave those places, those personal landmarks. How poignant are the images of home even if they are somewhat peculiar, like fainting in movie lines. My personal icons of home include those movie theatres where I received my mother's comfort and support. This is not an easy instruction to act on. Yet, in this phrase is contained the sanctification of the act of leaving one place and going to another. It is a positive direction, given by God to Abraham. In order for Abraham to discover the land God will show him, the deal is this: Abram and Sarai, plus his entire family, must leave.

To me, this Parsha is almost a mitzvah. It is certainly a mitzvah in the connotation of a worthy deed. This is an instruction that was to set the course of Jewish migration from one place to another, from that distant time of Abraham and Sarah right up to today. But there is a blessing here too. Perhaps a blessing in disguise. By moving from their lands, birthplaces and fathers' houses, Jews have oftentimes, and quite literally, saved their own lives. Hidden in plain view, this mitzvah of Abraham and Sarah can become the beacon for one who flees in fear and in danger to get to the border of the safe haven. Going from Spain to Portugal, from Europe to America, from Germany to Israel — these were ultimately life-saving escapes. And the blessing was, and still is, life! The blessing comes in the new lands.

Yet Lech L'cha can also be the words of sanctification to anyone who starts a new life, in a new place, with optimism and enthusiasm. My husband's grandparents fled Lithuania, settled in Leeds, chose a new life in Wisconsin and thrived in Beverly Hills. Their initial flight led to life for their children and grandchildren.

I am not the only student of Torah who takes this meaning from Lech L'cha. In The Torah A Modern Commentary, Rabbi W. Gunther Plaut observed that,

"For while Abraham's story must be read as the biography of an individual, he . . . is more than an individual. The Bible sees the Patriarch as the archetype who represents his descendants and their fate. He is the forefather, whose life hints at the later history of the people of Israel. This prefiguration begins when Abraham becomes a wanderer. Time and again his descendants will wander across the earth, along the highways of history."

Here is another example of leaving a life to create a new life:

The words of Lech L'cha are of particular poignancy,

to me, to my own life. Lech L'cha speaks to the person who flies, not fleeing in fear, but with arms fully extended, to embrace the entire Jewish tribe. Making this journey requires, absolutely and positively and voluntarily, that the candidate speak a solemn vow, witnessed by a Beit Din — a vow that is the equivalent of Lech L'cha, an affirmation to leave ". . . your land, your birthplace, your father's house . . ." And that is what I did as I stepped into my mikvah, embraced by the warm waters of transition, to emerge as Tovah Miriam. Lech L'cha jumps off the page for me.

I stepped into my mikvah, embraced by the warm waters of transition, to emerge as Tovah Miriam.

And here is a bit of real-life serendipity: Lech L'cha was the Torah portion that was being studied on the day I was born, October of 1945. Lech L'cha was to become the theme of my life. Its words were in the background, unbeknownst to me until very recently. And Lech L'cha resonates again with me now — loudly and clearly — now that I have left my land, my birthplace and, quite literally, my father's house.

Lech L'cha is the mitzvah of Jews in the diaspora and for any Jew who steps out of the waters of the mikvah, a stranger in a strange land. I did that. I left my land, that personal landscape of my childhood, with its quirky memories of going to the movies with my mother. I left my birthplace, my father's house — physically, metaphorically and truly. And my fainting in movie lines? Gone with the wind."

Non-Swimmer Considers Her Mikvah
More excerpts from
A Non-Swimmer Considers Her Mikvah

And then came my mikvah.

It was a requirement for my commitment to the continuity of Reform Judaism that I take a dip in the mikvah, an ancient symbolic ceremony which I would have to perform, in front of witnesses, as the sanctification of my decision. Along with the classes, the books, the study, the commitments and the solemn vows, Reform Judaism required that I had to immerse myself, in nakedness, into a mikvah pool, not once, but three times, to dip my entire head under the water, hair and all, and to lift up my feet from the bottom of the pool and to float under the water in a physical act of the sanctification of my new life. Everything which preceded the mikvah was a pure joy — the study, the books, the classes. And I was certain about my decision as I have not been about many other things in my life. But the mikvah drove more terror into my heart than the contemplation of God. I could not swim. I was afraid of water. Here I was about to become a stranger in a strange land and now they wanted me to dip into a strange substance as well!

And so I began to prepare.

My studio sink is a couple of feet in depth and I filled it with warm water. The water was clear and warm and salubrious. I gamely dunked, face first, into its depths. My exhaled breath sent big bubbles past my ears and water filled my ear canals. Pool deafness again. It was not too bad, but my head popped up completely on its own as I experienced my own reflexes of bodily panic. I was panting, gasping a graceless slurp of air. Head dripping, heart beating erratically, I thought about it. It is not the lack of conscious fear, it is not the sincerity of my determination, it is the involuntary reaction of my own nervous system that performs what looks and feels like fear of the water. I attempt two more dunks, each one more ragged than the first.

What I discovered in my studio sink experiments was not that I was afraid of water, but that my nervous system was. In theory, I was not afraid of anything. And, specifically, I was not at all afraid of my decision to become Jewish. But my imagination of the water engulfing me, filling my eardrums, deafening and surrounding me, alone as I would have to be in the mikvah pool; I feared most a kind of incomprehensible claustrophobia. I feared that I might panic in a spasm of my autonomic nervous system's fear of drowning. My fear was once removed from my rational self and from my more spiritual soul, but I was actually controlled by the uncontrollable automaton of my synapses.

Rationally, I viewed the waters of the mikvah as a final test of my commitment to the Jewish people, to the generations who came before me and with whom I was now committing my soul to join. After all, they had endured much worse than a pool of water.

Now the bargaining starts:

Maybe I could take adult swimming lessons at the JCC.

Maybe my Reform rabbi could give me a dispensation, after all we are Reform!

Maybe Moses could do that water-parting business again.

I Google mikvah: 680,000 results in .08 seconds.

Almost nothing for the non-swimmer. This is too humiliating.

Fear and anxiety grow in me. Breathless, I am having a real visceral anxiety attack. In feeling this anxiety, this beating of my heart, this irrational mind-chatter, this escalation of panic, I was experiencing my fear both in my head and in my body. How can I be so ridiculous?

Even I . . . I am embarrassed by my own cowardly, growing, stupid fear.

In yoga there is a concept of understanding one's soul through the careful observation of one's own body. By paying minute attention to our body, we can learn things about our mind, body, and soul. For example, by becoming fully conscious of muscles that we grip, we can know two things: 1) that we are, indeed, gripping them, and 2) that certain tensed muscles indicate certain internal spiritual or psychological states. Dipping into my sink I gripped my stomach and violently gripped and flexed my arms and legs and my heart muscle pumped jaggedly — all of these bodily responses happened without being volitional. All were physical expressions of fear.

And then I started to feel something new. It seeped into me, a little bit at a time, each day in the days before my mikvah. Perhaps my fear of water had given me a unique insight into what it is to be Jewish. I could not have understood the all-encompassing bodily response of fear without my own feelings of fear of water. Has not fear been with the Jews for thousands of years? The jackboots in the night. The fires of hatred. The pogroms. The camps. Make no mistake: I do not mean to diminish or trivialize the historic fears of the Jews with comparison to my own small irrational fear of being out of my depth in the mikvah.

On the contrary. The instinctive fear in my own autonomic nervous system demonstrated to me, vividly and personally, exactly how much beyond rationality fear can be — how automatically our arms reach out for support, our lungs gasp for air — how the breath of fear subsumes all other rational notions of life. But, surely, if the Jews could live through that, and other horrors unimaginable, I can do this. If Jews have survived these horrors, profound, unutterable, unceasingly in their repetition over generations, and now ingrained into the Jewish psyche, then surely — surely! — I can take my little fears and bear them into the waters of my mikvah.

And so, the day of my mikvah arrives. Afraid of water or not, today was the day I had to dive right in. Here I was about to become a stranger in a strange land and off I had to go into what was, for me, a very strange substance indeed.

I will do this.

The water is warm and it sparkles in the clear morning sunshine. My legs float out in front of me as the women of my Beit Din murmur instructions and encouragement. They ask me to close my eyes and visualize my life thus far. I see my mother's smiling face. I see Aunt B.'s smiling face. Their memories are, in this very moment, a blessing for me. Then my Beit Din asks me to visualize my future life as a Jewish person and I see a beautiful sunlit road winding into a distant clear sunny horizon. My heart knows I am doing the right thing. I feel uplifted. I dip into the warm water, face first, and feel — buoyancy!

I walk in Mary and step out Miriam.

I want to laugh. It is fine. I am fine. My hair floats for that first dip. Three more dips will be required. It is fine. Each dip is easier and more conscious than the one before.

Several things about the mikvah occur to me in these first few weeks I spend as a Jew:

- *The candidate has to go alone into the mikvah. This, I believe, is to ensure that I am acting by my own free will.*
- *The mikvah ensures the embodiment of a soul's desire to "dive into" Judaism. It is not so easy to discern a soul during its transition into Judaism. But the Beit Din can see it in the quality of the dive under the water.*
- *With the mikvah, I passed through one familiar earthly substance — water — and dove into a new and unfamiliar spiritual essence.*

You have kept us alive that we might live to this day.

On my fourth dip I plunge in, almost euphoric. I open my eyes under the water, lift my feet and feel embraced and buoyed by the water as the mikvah waters support me. Uncertain now, of only one last thing — that it might not be okay to laugh, to giggle — I stand up on the floor of the mikvah, aware of the grace of this moment, wanting to laugh out loud with happiness. On my fourth dip into the mikvah I am buoyant and euphoric, almost laughing, feeling laughter with my joyous euphoria.

"Did I do it? Did I do it?"

The women of my Beit Din were smiling,

"Yes, you did it! Yes!"

When I stepped out of my mikvah, it was as if the San Fernando Valley swimming classes had happened to someone else. Which, in fact, they had done. This is the fact of my mikvah experience. I walk in Mary and step out Miriam.

I did it.

2016

2018

2022

2024

2019

Of Particular Interest

One of my novels received unexpected accolades. No, that's not quite the right word for it. Reading aloud to a book group, I had an unexpected response from a handful of readers.

I was invited by a small library reading group to attend and to talk about my new novel *The Three-Day Departure of Mrs. Annette Zinn*. It had already received a very nice piece of literary acknowledgement with its WINNER sticker on its cover from the 2019 New Mexico-Arizona Book Awards.

The book group and I sat together at a library table and I had read aloud from my book.

Here is an excerpt from *The Three-Day Departure of Mrs. Annette Zinn:*

> *"This, her first grown-up job, working in that bookstore. Oh, treasured foolish aspiration. Bobbing at the ceiling of the bookstore, Mrs. Zinn watches it all unfold:*
>
> *Annette is shelving books. Paperbacks with their evocative scent of ink and paper and magical worlds to devour. She is so happy in her menial role in that little bookstore.*

The owner seems pleased with her work. He watches her as she scrabbles on her knees, stocking the lower shelves.

She stands up, a bit breathless from her efforts.

He, a man with thick white hair, maybe sixty or, if prematurely white-haired, he might have been only forty.

He walks up to her.

He stands still in front of her.

He does not speak.

He reaches out with both his hands.

He cups his hands around her jaws.

He gently — it will be recorded — takes her chin, gently, into his hands.

He moves forward to kiss her on the lips.

From her place in the world to come, Mrs. Zinn looks on.

Oh, poor little thing.

Poor me.

In a few years, this kind of entitled male aggression will be scandalously immortalized in literature. But for now, for the time being, this bookstore owner is no more than a sordid distant cousin, a libidinous ancestor, of the character who would emerge from that infamous book. On that day, in that bookstore, when Annette was just fifteen, this man was just a dog-eared, marked-down Humbert Humbert.

And that was that.

Annette had managed to get away somehow. Her guardian angel stepping between them. Or maybe it was simply quitting time. She escaped, yes. But never forgot.

"Fuck you, you fucking fucker," she said hovering from her vantage point in the world to come.

She liked the freedom of today's invective. She had never been shy of using it. Too bad she could not have used it then, when the white hair and the hands and those lips drew near to her little fifteen-year-old self. At fifteen, she had barely even known of the word "fuck". She saw it one time, knifed into the wood of a railroad tie. With a shiver, she had intuited it's meaning, even back then. . . .

Somehow little Annette had weaseled out of the man's grasp. And somehow, she had managed to weasel out of this, her first grown-up job.

What she told her mother was a series of obfuscations, not the truth. Never. Her mother, maybe wise enough to see through to the truth or maybe just too preoccupied to notice, her mother asked her:

"Was anybody in the store with you today?"

"No, Mama."

Then nobody saw it. It did not happen. Then her mother said:

"Let's go over to Bullock's and find that little tennis

> *bracelet you've been wanting. And, while we're there, let's get a bite to eat at the Tea Room."*
>
> *And, regardless of whether her mother was wise or simply expedient, she gave Annette the script: tell on him and you will be destroyed. Keep it to yourself and we'll go shopping.*
>
> *"Fuck the fucking fucker."*

But here is my unexpected reader response. Almost simultaneously, all four of the women in the library book group that I had been speaking with shouted:

"That happened to me!"

And what then took place was a rather emotional recounting of what, for these women, had been the same experience that I had narrated for my character, Mrs. Zinn. I may have even revealed that I, too, had had the same experience and that is how I wrote it into this, my novel. I hesitate to add that this admission turns out to support the dinner guest who asked me whether I wrote my novels from my own experience. Well, then. He wins. Right?

The only male in today's reading group got testy.

But there's more. The only male in today's reading group got testy. Ha! Nice pun, Carter! He got cranky and fidgety and was just this side of denying the truth of these four women readers. It was something to behold. All I wanted to do was to observe and take in the feelings darting back and forth across the table. The man: "just asking" as if somehow the women, remembering their teenage work experiences, were somehow not telling it like it really was. And wasn't it possibly true that — at this point — various book store managers were not *really* to blame. And we women all exchanged knowing looks, slight movement of our heads in denial. It was tense. It was unexpected, as I say. And a part of me was deeply gratified that I had been able, through my words and my fiction narrative, to touch the real lives of at least the female contingent of my readers on that day.

And that, THAT, was the very greatest honor for my fiction that I have received thus far.

Early Youth Not Yet Smart

In 1963 I was a freshman living in a girls dorm. My first foray into multi-girl daily life. Me, an only child. Good grief. What the heck did I know about my female peer group. I am certain I never used that word: Peer Group. Nevermind, what did I know of living with dozens of girls as we were called back then? No sisters. No brothers. An only child, stuck. I was living in my imaginary head, composing stories about people doing things. As if. And I never had an inkling of what rested in those many other girls' brains. Well, nothing like dorm living to almost instantly blow out any preconceived notions I may have had in September of 1963.

The first thing I was aware of, the very first thing that I witnessed, was two girls in a bathtub, one at either end. And when I went into the bathroom to take a shower, one of the girls opened the sliding glass bathtub door just an inch or so and peeked out at me. Softly closing that foggy door, they resumed whispering talk.

What the heck was that?

I didn't know what the heck what.

So blank. So stupid. So missing entire aspects of other young women's lives. Taking a bath. Together.

I tell ya. Nothing beats how under-protected I was back then. How naive. How really, and it's true: how stupid I was back then, just before my eighteenth birthday.

Then, worse, there is this:

One of the girls in our hallway was a very tough soccer player. In her floppy shorts one-piece overall, she ran, crashed, shoved, mutilated or just about, every single player on the other team. And she fell, crashed, rolled, then jumped up and did it all again and again and again. Not just once. But throughout the games.

I was stoned.
Still.
She was pregnant.
Just.

You know why don't you?

Certainly now.

But I was naturally clueless back then.

She was simply a type — an athletic showoff, more capable of gamesmanship than most of us girls, her teammates.

She had a name. Sherrylee.

And one day after lunch we streamed upstairs to our third floor hallway and one of the dorm doors stood open. Sherrylee's roommate was sitting on the edge of her bed on her side of the room. The other side of the room was empty. The bed rumpled, unmade. Sherrylee's roommate was near tears rambling that Sherrylee had been taken away by her father during lunch.

We never saw nor heard from Sherrylee again.

There was worse. That same freshman year, I am leaving Zoo with my heavy Zoology text clutched to my chest and this guy runs through the quad shouting: "The President's been shot. The President's been shot."

Well four years of dorm life was filled with what would become the best parts of my university education.

A girl rushes back from class. Slams the stall door in the bathroom and lets out a whoop of joy. It's here! Thank god!

A clutch of 'best friends' are quietly talking about a D&C she had at her doctor's office.

A friend of mine, Spanish major, did a year in Spain and her mother flew over there to spend some time with her.

There were no such dramatic moments between myself and my roommate during my Junior year. We lived in a room built for three, just us two. And it was an idyllic time. Yes. That's not an exaggeration.

Our time as roommates was a treasure to me. It was particularly so during Covid in 2020, as it trapped all of us at home. Plenty of time to reminisce. During that time I wrote *All Good Tova Goodman Revised Edition,* WINNER 2022 New Mexico-Arizona Book Awards. Here is an excerpt from that lovely time together:

> *Duck and Cover was the universal elementary school drill of their childhoods that would, supposedly, save*

their little asses when the atomic bomb dropped onto their playgrounds. That drill came right out of our parents' good war.

You do not grow up with Duck and Cover — heads under your desk with your little butt poking out into the aisle — without something deeply affecting you about this absurd, slightly crazy adult world. As a child growing up with Duck and Cover you cannot avoid noticing the very perversity of logic to the maneuver. This was supposed to save your life if an atomic bomb hit your school?

At ages six through eleven, you performed this little exercise, choreographed by the grownups. It hits you at your core, Duck and Cover, and at first you do not even notice it. You couldn't Duck and Cover to survive an atom bomb. Yet the grown-up's perverse life-saving maneuver surely hits you eventually and you get it: that you have been tricked. Lied to. Bamboozled by your parents. By your teachers. Maybe you don't consciously get what-the-heck it is, or was, until many decades later. How about that for existential fodder: your whole world — as it is told to you by the grownups — is absurd.

Teacher shouts:

"DROP!"

You drop.

You scramble your ever-longer legs under your desk,

despite knowing in your brain that this is futile; ridiculous. Children are not as stupid as they are sometimes thought to be. It surely was no darn good, this heads under the desk, butt in the aisle charade. And you knew it at age seven.

Good grief.

Tova muses to herself, "We were, Patty, the first-generation of Duckers and Coverers. And we noticed that, heads-under-desk-butts-in-aisle, was a charade."

That does something to you. Your first existential fallacy, yes?

It gave the roommates their wry, if not completely jaded, or completely bitter, world view. They had had it all their lives, ingrained. At age seven. Eight. Nine. Thirteen. Twenty.

Thus, by the time Tova and Patty were in college, they had developed a technique for dealing with this familiar branding from the parents: Bite the insides of your cheeks to keep from laughing. It is futile to argue with Duck and Cover.

The roommates had developed, during early childhood, a kind of cheery cynicism; that's what they had back then and that's what they would have, still, reaching age fifty.

Two very cute girls who shared a college dorm room built for three. They had a way to survive the adults who were raising us after their good war in the post-war sunshine, jubilant, materialistic, denial and plentitude of the fifties. Just bite the insides of your cheeks and don't scoff. It annoys the grown-ups.

Right now, Tova craves nostalgia. In contrast to her life right now, she needs to overindulge, to trip drunkenly, oblivious to all the troubles in her current world. A happy drunk; Tova runs her tongue along her snifter of nostalgia. Tastes of college, a mere four years. Not much of a span of time, as time goes. Really, nothing percentage wise, compared to the total of Tova's very long life. Nearing one hundred years of age, college will have been a very tiny percentage of the total.

It's so delicious. Looking back. Tasting such sweetness.

Spinning, barefoot, early spring on the campus grass, skirt lifting, a parachute, Tova glides in the sun, in that fragrance. Her rumpled term paper, pages breezy in the hot shade, sandals tossed, flung, on top of the document. There is an A- scrawled, hasty, across the cover sheet and one word scribbled alongside: Bravo!

At the end of their junior year, during Finals Week, Tova and Patty had much studying to do. But something tempted those two good girls to be bad. They decided to read aloud James Mitchener's very long novel, **Hawaii**.

Sitting on their high beds, first Patty reads a chapter

> *then Tova reads a chapter and they went back and forth like that until they got to the end of the 973 pages. Tova cannot remember how long it took them to read the whole thing. Maybe they pulled an all-nighter, which would not be surprising for Finals Week. Tova's memory is very clear, however, about taking turns to read aloud* ***Hawaii****.*
>
> *Tova grieves for such harmless transgressions. Today there are no such breaks in her life.*

Neither of us seemed to include existential meaning to our individual predicaments. We two roommates. We were so utterly imbued in the culture of the times. We indulged back then in what was just normal girlish chit-chat. She married just one week after my graduation.

Grudges Held From the Sexy Sixties

Born near the end of WWII, we were a wedge generation. Not boomers! Born a bit too soon for peace among nations. Born too late for the beginning of the women's movement. Never on its leading edge. Not being Boomers, we were the in-between-ers. We were brought up by mothers who vowed to love, honor and obey. But peace shoved at us a throbbing new potential for women. Sex. Drugs. University degrees. *Roe v. Wade.* We volunteered to be unshackled from love, honor, obey. We ran fast and loose, ready to fool around without getting knocked up. Brilliant! And within the very midst of this flailing fevered sexuality we did not notice that we were floundering. Still. We batted our eyelashes, weighty with mascara, to attract the 'men' we wanted. Men, being hardly an examined word nor an understood entity, in those early years of our freedom, so-called. We could not see that we were still working within the recognition and hoped-for approval of men. Competing for their over-valued attentions. To be pretty and sexy, we wore the shortest of short skirts. We went braless, flouncing our pretty sexy bosoms to one and all. We still responded to, and needed, the recognition and acclaim, the panting embraces, from the also-muddled minds of the newly 'freed' men. We fooled around. We were fooled indeed. Did any man we ever bedded, ever, ask us, after the task at hand – did they ever, later that same evening or even the next morning, over coffee, did a single man – free at last, free at last – did one of them ever ask for your thoughts on politics, religion, ethics, morals or any single thing of importance, so-called? Nothing had changed in our lives as women. Except the worry about pregnancy. Yet we played the same games and we were still being played. We did not notice that we were still playing at the same character we had always been, silent, withholding, secretive women only now you wouldn't get preggers. To love, honor, and obey. We were still doing it. Some progress! Between wars it was still all the same old, same old.

And we did not even notice.

But check out the real world that went booming on around us back then.

How 'bout art history?

Small example. Few college students ever dipped into that course. But look:

The text book between 1963 and 1967 was Jansen's *History of Art*. And the index did not include the names of a single woman artist. And we did not even notice.

Not until decades, literally, later did any of us who had

taken Art History — capital A capital H — even remember those years, when Jansen was our textbook, and that not a single female was included in that exposition of art history.

You say I quibble.

I take umbrage.

Or how bout this one: I got a divorce in 1971 and sitting at yet another long table, his attorney, my attorney, they asked me to bring out my MasterCard and my Union Oil credit card and to cut them into pieces because, as an unmarried woman, I would not be able to use my credit cards any more. Nor could I obtain new ones, unmarried. Cards I had earned by being employed myself all through that measly little marriage, by the way. Not mine any more. And, irony of irony, the Ex had to sign a landlord's document that I could be trusted to pay the rent when I obtained my own apartment.

And when I asked the attorneys if I could return to my *maiden name* that the Ex's attorney warned me:

"Well you can use your maiden name again just so long as you don't use it to commit a crime."

What-the-heck!!!

And, right there and then at the divorce proceedings, and sadly unbeknownst to my limited consciousness of that era, I was right then and there having my self stifled, my name belittled, my tongue bound for my presumption in wanting to have it returned to me — my own surname — for what little I deserved after breaking the sanctity of marriage, so-called.

The bindings were brutal. Subtle, but bruising. Take that, you presumptuous little girl.

These are just small examples from my life as a liberated woman, so-called. Not a Boomer, not. I have serious beefs about these kinds of things now that I am about to turn eighty.

> *"Well you can use your maiden name again just so long as you don't use it to commit a crime."*

I wish I had noticed these things sooner. An index with no women. Being instructed to cut up my credit cards in front of my Ex and two attorneys: MasterCard and Union Oil. And then, a self-righteous admonishment to me about not committing a crime when or if I resumed my maiden name.

Oh, yes. I hold many grudges from this vantage point of age and experience. And what, pray tell, does all this have to do with how on Earth we talk? Well you ask. We each of us — no matter what era we are born into — reveal what we have borne during those times. All of those events — wars, famines, politics, travel — all of our background lives will reveal ourselves to others in the words we select to speak with one another.

Ever the Girlfriend

Ah, but what about love? Luv? We are already so many pages into this book and there's not a single rumpled sheet. Patience, I caution. We will get there. It takes a certain amount of bravery — bravado — to succumb to love. Sometimes you need to be as brave as perhaps you saw that I was during my encounter with a man with a gun. No. Brave is not precisely the right word for how you have to be when you fall in love. Especially when you are young and subject to overwhelming waves of love. Love upon love. First this guy. Then that guy. Then again, it's even more distracting, this love thing, with yet another guy. Ah, yes. What indeed about love? Over and over again, the girl falls in love. Foolish girl. You will actually become a fool, once you fall, tumble, crash and burn, with love.

We who are too-old today are suddenly aware that, back then, we were simply too uninformed to see through our own naiveté. We did not know how to know better when it came to love. We gratefully stepped into our pharmacies to buy our pills, but we did not have a clue as to what that freedom would entail. For all our liberation we were trapped inside our same old muddled concepts about how we needed to lure men into our lives. Same old, same old ideas about how we needed them and much of it came down to our looks — our pretty knees showing below teeny skirts. Our long curling locks, blowing seductively in the Santa Ana Winds. Our silences inside classrooms, even in college we were silent and didn't notice the silence toward young women. In college Art History, you would not learn about Mary Cassatt or even that old lady artist, Grandma Moses. We were still trying to love, honor, and obey so we did not speak up, we did not even notice how our silence was enforced all around us, even in college.

And so her name is Nina. Friend of mine, back then. A nice flirty sort of name for a girl who fell and fell, in and out of love, again and then again. Listen to her small story. It's all about love in 1965:

"That's me. Nina Yablonsky. I may have made some timid progress in my management of my love affairs. But it's for certain: I never had a single conversation about any single thing that was important to my soul with men back then. Never a single word from that latest Harry Handsomsides. He bounced up, dressed up, sped off in his car, out into the world to do important things. I changed the sheets."

Foolish girl.

Speak Up, Girls!

What follows is a short story. It is all fiction for this chapter, featuring a character who is a deft fictional person: Katrina. I created her. How and what she speaks is fiction. Based upon my life? We shall see. Katrina enables me to articulate, more clearly, with greater intensity, my feelings after hearing wicked gossip way back when.

Uh-oh.

It's Kat.

She hasn't said a word. Yet. But she stirs. She groans, a muffled throat clearing sort of sound, a kind of buried sigh or a groan stuck deep in the back of her tongue. This will be good. Kat is as direct as her nickname, virtually spits her words out. No doubt about Kat. When Kat speaks, she can be as terse as her monosyllabic moniker. But you always know, it's gonna be good when Kat pipes up. Our favorite loudmouth.

Well, it's me speaking. Listen up ladies. It's me, first person singular. Katrina! Pay attention if you please.

How on Earth do we talk? Why on Earth ask? And why on Earth do we try to write about how we talk? Or talk about how we talk? It's crazy, really. Right?

Yes. That's the best question: Why on Earth do we talk about how on Earth we talk?

But listen here. The cat's out of the bag. THIS Kat's out of her bag. Listen up, ladies.

You were much too gentle, too courteous, Mary, when you spoke of gossip both the noun and the verb. But you are too gentle, Mary. How 'bout using the word cunt? You are too careful. You edit out too many other such offensive words from your account of that hurtful bit of gossip. Gossip that killed something in you, Mary. And I'm not just singling you out, Mary. Each of you toned down your heart-breaking stories. Elizabeth, you could have screamed at the authors of that ratty little VA brochure about Agent Orange. Torn up that fucking brochure right in front these readers. That would have told the real story. That tidy informational brochure from our own Veteran's Administration – so called – that just cleverly, diabolically never mentioned that your beloved soldier was going to die from his exposure to Agent Orange in Vietnam. Or you could have sent the VA a scathing letter. Mary, you tell and repeat your story of the man with a gun – two guns, actually – in your synagogue parking lot. Hey, girl! That was wild and crazy and brave and foolish and it was, and is, beyond words, mere. You should have been able to fire home and on target other words to drive home your bravery that day. But you did not. You wrote nice clean words and left out anger, invective, power.

See what I'm getting at here?

We women tell our stories — yes we do — but we hold back. Make it nice and clean. We are courteous even mildly humorous about our most excruciating experiences. I say, come on Girls. Get a grip. Speak up. Yell. Throw something. Never Forget. Right? You did that part. But you must do this too: Never Forgive.

And I might add, Never Edit. You are all much too guarded in your speech, ladies. Much too much. Much of a muchness. And why do you still strive to sound so lady-like? What's the point in that, my friends? You want to sound 'proper'? Well let me inform you — each of you is old enough to know better — there is no such thing as speech that is ladylike. Don't even try. Speak up!

Are we just a little bit reminded of Mary's Commentary about Sarah in the Akedah? How she either did or did not speak up? Or was Sarah perhaps edited out of *Torah* by the Redactors? So how does Sarah's lack of words relate to how Mary tells her story?

In addition, I could say, you were much lacking in common useful Bullshit Detection. Let me tell you all a thing or two about how you all talk about your pivotal life-killing events that you just told us about. Your language was just too clean.

Too gentle. Too — are you still worried about how you sound — too like the ladies you have always strived to be. You are still striving to sound ladylike. You even retell events with somewhat mordant humor.

Feh!

Well wait just a damn minute. I am not so concerned. Never have been. Always speak my mind and bedamned the outcome. So now, I shall speak for each one of you. I shall be your outspoken loudmouthed redactor. I shall speak for you. Edit out your niceties. Get straight to the point. And not mince words.

Yes indeedy-do: How on Earth do we speak? Some of us speak through me, Kat. That's me. You bet. So listen up you bunch of too-old ladies. I have plenty more to say.

Let me tell you a thing or two. Words, *mere*, can and do kill these days. Words also may end you up in court. Accused of — now let's see — slander, libel, accessory to murder? And words, *mere*, can get you killed. Think 'free speech'.

Now there's the latest actionable form of wordplay. Nowadays you can be shot by some illiterate slob, his fat thighs spreading wide open as he types into his grimy laptop. He, who takes offense at your being a loudmouth female, speaking your mind, in opposition to that slob's favorite and beloved and rankly evil occupant inside the latest public office. That slob, influencer they call him these days, can get it in his brain to go after you and look: you are shot. For speaking out. How on Earth do you talk to a slug like that? But the result of your unguarded words may end you up dead. Just as dead as if you died of a random nonjudgmental case of germs, *mere,* namely vicious cancer that speaks not a single word. But no. Those shouted bits of free speech, so-called, can get you brutally killed.

And so, sadly my ladies, you withdraw your spoken words — whether just talk or written in brilliant screed-form — you step back and clean up your words just in case your freedom of speech gets dangerous.

I urge you to speak up. Stop editing. Stop equivocating.

There's more here: listen.

Now, this current bugaboo, free speech, can literally get you arrested, placed in chains and wearing an orange jumpsuit for your next snapshot. A snapshot, plus mind you how you speak, it will be placed in quote marks right alongside your snapshot in orange. It will be a snapshot that will circle the globe, the entire Earth, in seconds, *mere*, all around our fetid globe from stinking websites operated by many devils incarnate who label themselves 'influencers'. And it will be words, *mere,* that you hear from your accused chair at your defendant's table, in a real live courtroom filled with your accusers who have no moral or ethical centers, but who are well educated indeed as attorneys for the prosecution, pressing you with the charges of actionable speech, of libelous speech, and in the end, of free speech, *mere*, as well.

You like that? You think you may say whatever you want? Think again. How on Earth may you speak and remain free? It's a conundrum. It's made that way so that you will hesitate whenever you utter somewhat volatile yet 'free' speech, so-called. It can get you killed.

We have been given literary conventions, each with its own style and rules: Fiction, Memoire, Historic, Scientific, Non-Fiction, Biography, Auto-Biography, Romance, Mystery, Poetry, Detective novels. Gossip.

We are given many useful tools, the aptly-named 'givens' for book writing: Narrative Arc, Plot, Back-story, Climax, Denouement. And more than 'tools', prescribed ways of handling 'fiction' are so pesky, so ingrained at times, that, without much willpower on the part of the author, this author perhaps, or you, Mary, we grab onto these tools, along the way as we write our stories, as we talk our stories into being — suddenly we are slaves to the need to use these tools to identify for our readers or listeners, where, exactly, we are headed with our talking. How on Earth do we write?

How on Earth do we talk?

With all of these preconceived notions of how to handle the writing about our lives, summing things up at an advancing old age, we are, in a sense, hamstrung into conviviality as proper ladies, speaking our minds. When we actually speak. Yet our speech is truncated by female propriety. We don't shout. We don't remonstrate. We just sit there and take it. Like Sarah? I wonder. I'm talking about wicked gossip. Gossip is always aimed in careful attack-mode. Whether written or spoken, we must balance preconceived decisions for the listener, or reader, of said gossip, to never respond this way or to only respond to it that way. And why? Why I ask? In the case of Mary's narration about a cruel gossip – I would go further and call that woman gossip a pervert. A creep. A psychopath. Yes? A psychopath bent on harming a grieving young woman, you Mary, and making her bleed. And we women know a lot about bleeding, don't we?

I almost forgot: it's called Lashon Hara. I prefer the words Lashing Horror. That's what that form of speech is. Gossip. Aimed point blank. Murderous in its intention and in its aim.

My heart does indeed bleed for our friend Mary. It is shocking. It is vile. That woman who told Mary all about what her real life had been as the daughter of a man, a pervert, her parent, – it is beyond words. Isn't it? It is so creepy and weird for that gossip – the woman who told the tales to Mary – words fail. And right then and there Mary should have, but could not have, shouted at her tormenter. That's indeed what and who that gossip was. Sitting there on Mary's mother's upholstered chair in Mary's home –former – now that her mother was dead. Mary could even have taken physical hold of that woman, that gossip, and slapped her bloody over this wanton destruction of all of Mary's previous perceptions about her family that was killed the moment the gossip finished her story, graphically illustrated with back-alley jargon, the moment those words were out of her mouth and fired at Mary. She had all the moral and ethical rights to have beaten that woman shitless. None of us would argue. Mary had the rights. But she lacked the guts. Instead she turned the graphic content of that gossip into another blow of death to her own self. Mary died too, if that is even possible, when she heard those words of that vicious dirty gossip.

How on Earth do we talk? Sometimes with venom, intent upon harm. Words fail.

Uh-oh.

So, right now, it's me speaking, Katrina. Call me Kat.

During lunch yesterday with three 'too-old ladies' – friends of mine – I kind of, sort of, vaguely, stumbled upon an aspect of how on Earth I speak among my friends. Mostly I have, over the years, kept my stories to myself. The stories, in particular, the episodes from my life that I had thought were too ugly, too weird, too negative to speak of out loud with various types of women friends of mine – I did not talk about those stories. Secretive I was? Yes, but in addition, I have often been afraid that if I told some of my stories, that people would be disgusted or put off by my candor, or would not want to be near somebody that talked about such things. Talking about grief was one such topic. Using the word 'death' another. Our culture prefers pseudonyms for death like: passed, or passed away. Like vapor? Never. We're talking death. Say it: she's dead.

But also these: talking about certain kinds of familial disfunction, to my mind, can seem, well, unseemly. And my underlying fears have been that if I touch on these kinds of personal and hurtful things, friends would flee from me. Ugh! Kat's just too weird. She takes it all too personally. She's just too sensitive. That's a fault? God! How did she ever survive those things when her loved one passed?

She died, gawdamnit.

And that's what happened to Mary when the gossip struck.

And Mary had every right to beat that gossip into fucking death.

There are plenty of ways to lose a friend. And my friendships — if I revealed too much about myself I thought — might have been provisional to those around me all because of my being secretive or withholding of actually telling my stories. I have been afraid of that. How on Earth do we talk when we are fearful? I have often thought that most of my friendships would be posited upon my being cheery, humorous, entertaining, but never completely open and honest, god forbid. That's it.

How on Earth do we talk? In my case it is, rather, how on

Earth do I survive and hold friendships if I talk too much, if I am too truthful about hurtful things? If I use sharp pointed rhetoric?

The largest anxiety that I have, me, Kat, as a person, and that I have toted around with me as I have gradually dipped into becoming an author of sorts, is that I would push people away from me when, or if, I told real truths in blunt words. And there are so many such moments, times when I chose to NOT talk in the first person so as to keep the friends that I had. Or so I thought.

I equivocate more often than not. For safety. So that I do not shock and scare away my friends. It has only been with a select few — count them on one hand with a missing finger — that I have dared to do otherwise.

> *Katrina, my fictional character here in this short story, helped me to speak more pungently about the effects of the gossip on me.*

Yet now, right here, hear how I have gradually begun to reveal my own voice. Been lured back into using my own words. Dared to let pseudonyms drop. Or perhaps a better descriptor: I have been tempted back into using my own speaking voice.

How on Earth do I speak? Is this me, Kat? Or Mary speaking?

I'm gonna speak up right this minute for Mary. Right now. With a bit more detail around some of the cruel bits and shards in Mary's lifetime as the daughter of a man who told Mary that she was the one who had been in the way of all the things he had wanted to accomplish during his entire life up to now. He told Mary this as they were driving aimlessly around in his car, just two days before her mother's funeral. If she had not been grieving so grievously at that death – say it – then what he laid on her when Mary innocently asked how come he had not done all those things he had wanted to do in his life? His response? He could have shoved Mary right out of that car, into blank oblivion. Ten years later, Mary told her shrink all about those sparse five words, spoken by that man:

"Because you were always there."

Five sparce words. Death.

Her shrink asked her, quickly with intuitive and professional focus:

"Then what did you do?"

And she responded, lickety-split,

"I killed myself."

Ah. There. A breakthrough. See? It's not just the words. It's who and how, and even when, it is said.

I do believe that Mary feared that she must have somehow deserved those five icy words flung at her just two days before her mother's funeral. Delivered by the master of Zero-Sum love. Love her or love me type of guy. Take your pick. Ya can't love us both. From her father, The Pilot, always in control, at his controls.

What the shrink and Mary gradually dug out was that for a decade Mary had resided, quite dead, in a fugue state. Mary, high-functioning in each of her jobs, had been deeply buried, blinded to her truer self. She had not painted for ten years. Mary, the art major in college. Nothing. Not a stroke. She had done nothing creative for a decade except to show up at work. Perform well. Go home. Her resume grew and flourished, each job a substantial rise above the last one. Her bosses glowed with compliments for her superior performances. Advertising copywriter she was. Big bucks now at last on Mary's paychecks. Tastes Great.

Then she one night woke up screaming, terrified. Night terrors had begun.

After the breakthrough with her shrink, she came home and curled up on the sofa, snoozing. Gary came up to her with a small pat and asked: "Did he open up Pandora's Box?" Indeed that was what was done. Stay away from Kat. She's a real bummer. She will say what's not been said.

But now, I will say what has not been said. I will tell it all. Tell it true. To my own nervous credit, I have still withheld the exact words of the woman who fed Mary the gossip at that ill-timed holiday gathering nearly a half century ago. Let me further remind you, dear reader, that the gossip and her gossip hit Mary on the first Christmas party after her mother's death on September 30th 1968. The timing of the attack could not have been more horrifying, filled with Lashing Horror. Yes. Indeed it was. Take my word for it, the gossip's words were vile. Her words hit Mary, blindsided her and shocked her and devastated her and with a stroke of her tongue, that gossip and her gossip destroyed all of Mary's preconceived notions about how her family had been throughout her own childhood. Done with. In a stroke of cruel dirty words. Well I say: quit with the ladylike words. Raise your hackles. Shout, Girl! Throw out some of your own dirt:

"Fuck you, you fucking fuckhead."

It sounds kind of funny doesn't it.

The famous F-word doesn't have the heft it used to have back in the day. Well, we can try can't we? It's still just no good to try to rationalize the kind of gossip, the person, with the gossip, the verb – that literally changes a life, causes life-changing harm. Turns a young woman's soul into dust. Worse. Worse. It's hard and impossible to figure out how on Earth to talk.

How on Earth do we talk? It can be just like that.

Mary never forgot. Mary never forgave. That's her story.

I am stepping up to retell Mary's story. The parts she did not speak. Like her choice of the *Torah* portion, the Akedah, Mary latched onto Sarah, perhaps recognizing a kindred soul whose tongue was tied as knotted as Mary's did become. And so, this Matriarch, Sarah, became for a time, Mary's matriarch. Perhaps. And from this matriarchy came Mary's midrash, later elevated to being Commentary about women whose tongues were bound. Funny how *Torah* study works. Yes? How on Earth do we dare talk? Talk talks. Silence too.

Breaking Through the Silence of my Fugue.

Meanwhile, back to my first person, author's narratives in this book. This is my recollection of the moments of my life immediately after I awoke from my fugue state.

Almost literally waking from my silent fugue, after a short afternoon nap next to Gary, I woke up, rushed upstairs to my desk, and started to draw. Breaking through my decade of silence, I started again and, working furiously, I rushed images onto old scraps of paper, whatever came to mind. I was awake again. I started to speak again through a pile of drawings I made that very afternoon. Soon I would buy several stretched canvases and pots of paint and off I went. No more silence. Just energy. Force. I was again creating images. And those images were worth words after so long a silence. I was regaining who I had been, during those years of college as an art major, graduating at last, hearing for the first time Marc's question:

"What are we going to do now, Mary Carter."

That indeed. Finally. Silence broken. Fugue diminishing. Then gone. I had a lot to say and said it thus:

This image is from 1979:

Gone, too, and importantly, was my desire to continue as an advertising copywriter. I gave my notice to Grey Advertising management after three years in that office. Management urged me to stay on, bribed me with promotion, money, flattered my work, promised to keep my job for me if or when I decided to return. But I was on my way back into my studio. My motivation to paint was almost frenetic and my energy was very great. I had a lot of time to make up for. I had a lot to 'say'. Interestingly to me was how much the work, those first few months of paintings, looked like the kind of work I would have been doing if I had stayed in my studio and painted for all those years immediately after graduation. That is, my skills as a painter had somehow 'developed' during my absence from doing that work. My new paintings showed a degree of progress in brushwork, style, drawing, and concept that I might have gotten to if I had kept painting after 1967.

"What are we going to do now, Mary Carter?"

Every morning I went into my studio at 7:00 AM and worked until time for lunch which was announced to me when Kitty Priester leaped silently up onto my worktable. There she would sit, on the edges of whatever image I was creating, and she would purr a bit when I reached out to pat her. She was hungry. She wanted me to make lunch for us. I might not have noticed the time had it not been for KP.

An Exquisite Corpse, Not Yet Dead

Artist Statement From my Website: www.mary-carter.com:

From my early award winning graphic paintings of the 1980's through to my complex atmospheric and metaphorical works of 2007, I have created a vocabulary of images and a stylistic signature for my contemporary surrealism. Flying, falling and floating through my work are goose girls and chicken ladies, cigarette-smoking brides, entwined lovers, and inadequately winged creatures.

My work is contemporary figurative surrealism. I say "contemporary" because I want to put distance between my painting and the manifestos of the Surrealist painters of the first part of the 20th Century. Yet as to that state of mind, that ineffable dream, that flow of metaphor and symbol, that unlocking of the subconscious, I identify with those sources of visualization.

Process: My Solitary Search for the Exquisite Corpse

The historic Surrealists experimented with a drawing technique called Exquisite Corpse. A piece of paper was folded into several sections. A small group of surrealists would gather and each one, in turn, would add figural elements to a single section of the folded paper. When each section was folded, it was out of sight and no other artist could see what had been filled in before. Each artist would draw in figural elements without seeing what the other artists had created. This 'game' resulted in a montage of a figure, sometimes humorous, sometimes weird, always perversely beautiful, expressive, and always creative beyond rationality. These new drawings tweaked preconceived notions of what was 'right' or 'correct' in art.

But, most importantly, the exercise was done as an aid to unlocking the subconscious minds of the artists. The resulting figure was the Exquisite Corpse. These exquisite drawings revealed sometimes hilarious, sometimes eerie things about the human condition and provided a door to images from the collective unconscious of the artists in that group. The drawings rearranged expected patterns and in wonderfully bizarre forms, tweaked preconceived notions of how art is actually made.

Similarly, I start with the human figure in my work. But I work alone. My paintings grow as much out of my interaction with the human form as from pure intellectual processes or rationales, growing as much from my hands working as from my brain thinking. My aim is to open the doors of my own perception in order to access my own subconscious and preconscious material and to challenge my own notions of artistic correctness. I start by drawing a naturalistic human form on paper. Then I cut it apart, reassembling limbs and organs, adding or subtracting elements until new patterns of human possibility emerge. I prepare the canvas separately, splashing, sloshing, or dripping paint on the raw surface. Despite allowing paint its way at this stage, there is nothing expressionistic about my backgrounds. Gradually I reign in my surfaces, meticulously re-working them, inch by inch, to create an atmospheric depth into which my figures will fly, float, or fall, communicating their ineffable ambiguous tales. These figures speak to me. Finally, I place the drawing over the canvas ground and use elements of the ground to further shape and influence the drawing of the figure as I paint it into its atmosphere. By shifting anatomical elements I create an exquisite corpse. Yet, far from dead, this vision is alive in its unfamiliarity. Emotionally compelling, my figures reveal sub and preconscious states of humanness. My work acts as a Rorschach test. Sometimes people see different things in it from my intentions. But even when viewers do not see what I may have had in mind when I worked on a painting, there is a certain logic to their perceptions. And who knows? Maybe those Rorschach reactions are, indeed, what my work more inclusively intends.

End of quote from my website: www.mary-carter.com

Can you imagine what a ten year hiatus of creative work means? How it feels from the inside, then the outside, of the artist? The writer? In my life for the entire decade immediately following 1968 I made not ONE drawing, sketch, or painting. Not a mark on canvas or paper. I wrote not a single creative word outside of the words of advertising that were required by my profession. Tastes Great!

But what is baffling to me is that when I experienced my breakthrough — when I answered my shrink's question to the snide accusation that I had been the one at fault for all of another person's sacrifices, that I had been to blame because I had been a burden and that:

"You were always there."

And my shrink asked me:

"Then what did you do?"

I shot back a swift response:

"I killed myself."

That was news to me.

I had not even known, never even suspected, that I had NOT been painting. Not been writing. I had not articulated through language or through insights, that I had done such damage to my creativity that it was like another death after the death of my beloved mother. When I said those words, I sprang up, metaphorically, yet I actually did jump out of my seat and I yelled a kind of girlish halleluiah, my answer revealed that:

It was I who had been had been an Exquisite Corpse.

My first image that I created was on a little office pad that had my name on it. It was a figure with a hand pressed against an object — a wall or something — in a gesture of pushing back. I gave that little drawing to my shrink so I do not have it any more. But here is a sample of how that gesture occurs often in my work.

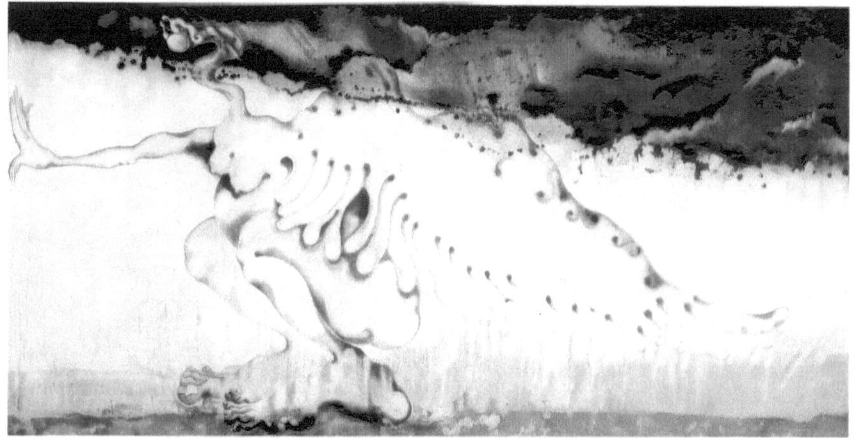

After ten years of silence, I could speak again. And I have done so. And I continue to do so. Stand in my studio, view my paintings, listen to my voice. And here's another thought to consider: Does an artist **speak** through the images they put onto canvas and paper? Do ALL artists use this medium — paint and brushes and substrates — as vehicles for how on Earth they speak? Here is a recent painting of mine and I ask you, does it speak of my mikvah? In so doing, I realize that converting my experience into a painting sounds good to me. By this conversion of my mikvah experience that word conversion does not sound so negative to me. Converting my mikvah experience into a painting sounds okay now to me. The only usage of the word 'conversion' that I can now tolerate.

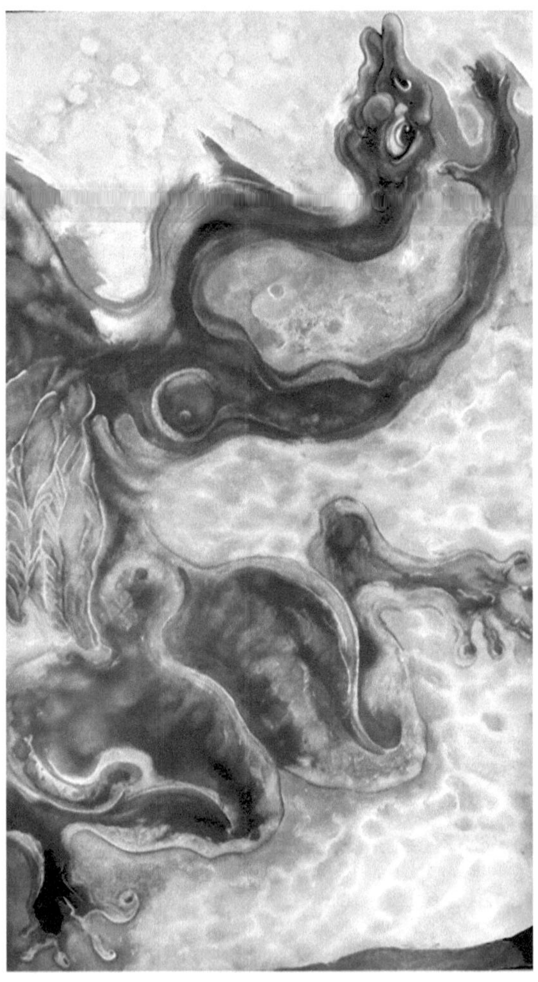

Pool 2011

Early 80s paintings from my Snapshot series.

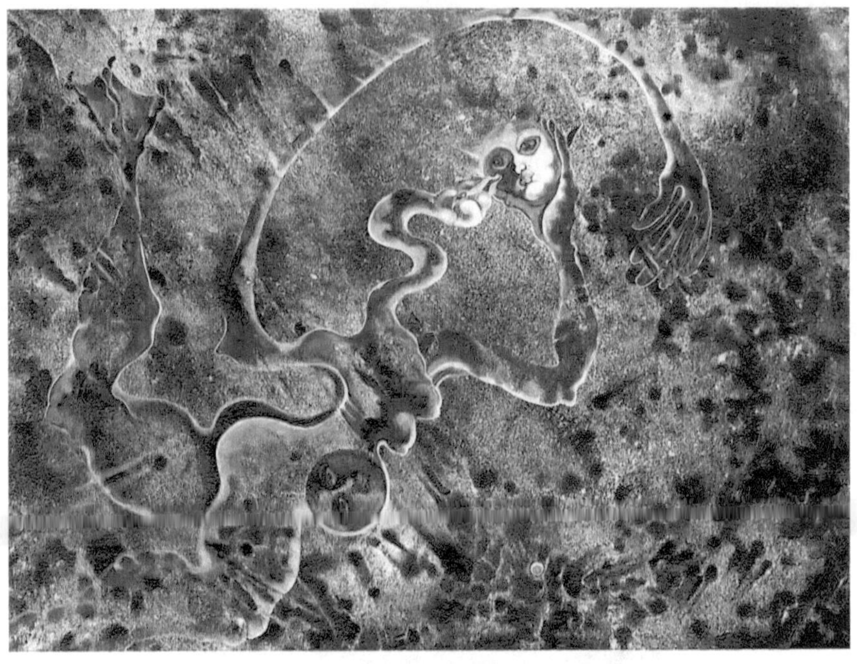

Recent paintings from my Guardian Angel series.

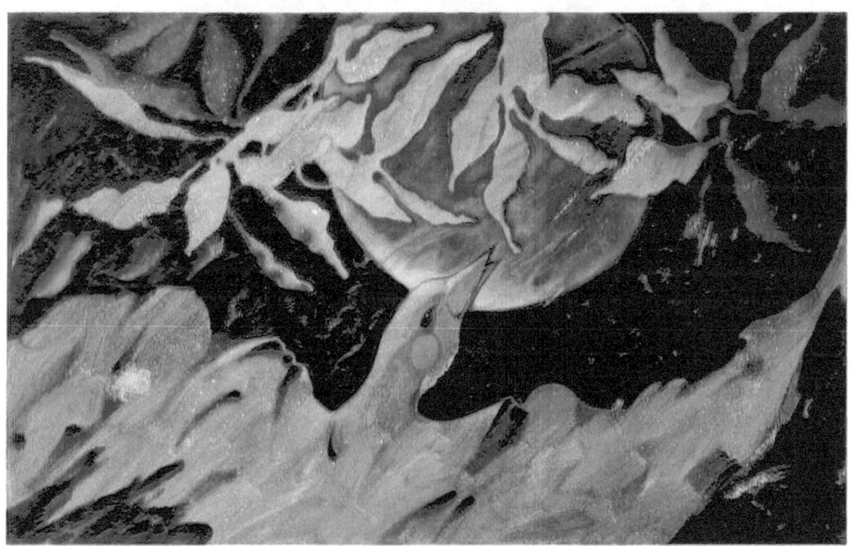

Recent paintings from my Blackbird series.

May I Speak Right Out loud?

We begin each morning immerged and embraced by words. Seated in a room not much larger than eight feet by ten feet, it is protected by a flamboyant patterned rug — Oriental? — with its elaborate edges revealing a border of shiny bare red floor tiles. Along this border rest enormous — yes they are looming, heavy — bookshelves that are bound to the walls with L-brackets, screwed into the very wallboards. The shelves are that heavy and that top heavy that if not thus tightly bracketed, they would tilt forward until crashing onto our chairs. Causing injuries, no doubt. Maybe even death. So surrounded by, how many, a thousand? — books and books and books and I wondered the other morning: why?

Gary and I are sipping our hot brew of black coffee from our cheery yellow and red cups. We are about to start our morning read — aloud. We have been reading aloud every morning and every evening for at least 35 years. Usually fiction for mornings. Non-fiction, evenings.

Why on earth write down all those billions, yes billions, of words and put them into permanent forms, between cardboard covers, on pages and pages and pages of typeset words? Why such human effort to put words onto all these permanent and solid objects? And ours, here in a tiny library, are only a fraction. There are billions of these products, books and books, out there in the world. Shelved or tossed onto what must be ever more bracketed shelves for books. And why do I turn to them, with an odd randomness, in the thrall of random moods, why do I turn to, say, a book about cats or a book about surrealism or a book about a contemporary of mine who is a Brit and who writes fiction about British angst so urgently? How come? I am the customer for all these words and words and words. I cleave them and place them in my home on enormous clumsy shelves. Why not just sell them in a massive garage sale? Dump them? Give them away. What's the point of keeping all these words? Why on Earth do we speak? On and on and on?

So I begin each day surrounded by words. Speech. Talk. How on Earth does this work and why? And why put all those words onto paper?

And then, as the mind over a cup of hot black brew, my mind, flashes on a connection: Am I Sarah? Tongue-tied? Bound? Captured by her story in her Akedah? In a way, perhaps I muse egotistically, I am not unlike Sarah in that I have given birth to many words in my latter years. Given birth to the offspring of my paintings and of my fiction in solid objects, books, when I, too, am an old woman giving birth to my beloved creations when well past my fertile years. Like Sarah? So when I read it, the Akedah, I shout at it in frustration and in recognition of a tongue bound by yet other words. Sarah. In frustration that, I too, have never spoken my mind. My heart. My feelings, most true. And thus I identify, instinctively, with Sarah's silence. That was like my silence, too. Sarah is not quoted in the Akedah as saying nor responding to any thing. And I jump, startled. Yes, that was me, too. After the gossip from the gossip, I shut down. After The Pilot said:

"You were always there."

Slapping his hands on the steering wheel, shouting almost, but spitting too as we drove around aimless now, two days before my mother's funeral. Oh I could shout: **For Godsakes!!** Those were words of erasure, words to nullify my past existence as his so-called beloved child in this little family. Not so. And I shut down. Not treasured. Then, lapsed into a fugue state. Shut up. Benighted, I moved on? Yes, I did indeed move on. I got new jobs. Was a moderate success. Never missed a day's work. But I was silent. Gone. And it could easily have been said: And Mary died . . . But I had not realized it at the moment of those words. Not until seeking therapy after a decade and motivated by night terrors, then, finally, I woke from my fugue and my life took on an entire new narrative. I woke up.

In gatherings like today, seated around what we may call our Talking Table, with several women friends, all of us too-old, having lunch together. Laughing, joking, speaking out. I speak with lightness, wise-cracking, or skimming the surface of my innermost thoughts, a light-hearted friend, surface oriented. Me. Safe company in a group of my friends. But listen to this: When I speak my mind out loud I may well hear in response:

"You shouldn't be so sensitive. What do you care what happens to your cats after you die? You'll be dead."

Nice.

Those words were hurtful to me. Stung. It became a repeated phrase from several friends. But it became my warning. Do not speak to anybody about what you most truly cherish in your heart, my love for each of our cats, these I worry about. What if, for instance, I and Gary both die simultaneously? What will happen to our kitties? Who will take good and loving care of them? But do not reveal this nagging anxiety. That I worry about what will happen to my cats after I die. Well, so be it. But don't mention it again to anybody.

But forget it? No.

But the result is that I now withhold my words. How on Earth do we speak with the reins of certain speech held firm? Bind me. The reins of other people's opprobrium? Sometimes, as witnessed in the work of the Redactors of the Akedah, we, and by 'we' I mean I — I speak using no words. I say nothing. It's safer that way. Say nothing.

What if Sarah had reacted with throwing a dish at Abraham, would some righteous soul have said to her:

"You shouldn't be so sensitive. What do you care what may have happened to your son? You'll be dead."

And sure enough. All that was left to be said about Sarah in the Akedah was:

"And Sarah's life was a hundred and twenty-seven years, the years of Sarah's life."

All that Sarah revealed or received was silence. There is no speech from her lips. There is no narrative description about how Sarah reacted when Abraham and Isaac came home.

"And Sarah's life was a hundred and twenty-seven years, the years of Sarah's life."

That's all folks. That's it? We are taught, by inference, from Redactors perhaps, NOT to react. NOT to be so sensitive. To abide? Perhaps. The Akedah during the High Holy Days is set as an example of 'sacrifice'. But sacrifice of what? Of whom? But it is crystal clear from the narrative of the Akedah, Sarah says no thing. Not a thing. Thus it is more her sacrifice I hear. Her sacrifice of speech. She has none. Her sacrifice of her reaction to Abraham and Isaac within the narrative: Sarah says no thing. Certainly not a word about 'sacrifice.'

In the Akedah, Abraham gets speaking lines. Isaac gets a bit. Certainly not Sarah. Sarah is not given speech. But, upon probing, we may decide that she is NOT speaking which is a perverse way of saying, she said no thing. Which subtly tells the engaged *Torah* student: there are moments NOT to speak.

But let's get back to books.

The permanence of books may speak to us when we re-read them. It may be that we have changed just enough to 'hear' new meanings. And then, quixotically, we may receive different messages from our books during different stages of our lives. And we may grok completely different things held within battered old paperback books, dragged in boxes from one apartment to the next. For decades. And so, those old volumes may speak to us on widely different occasions. And, surprisingly, we may say:

"Wow. I never noticed that before."

And so, books speak to us not only at different times, but also books may contain new messages that we never may have noticed before. Maybe we could not have understood certain passages because our lives had not reached the point where we could notice what a certain book was 'saying'. And so books, sitting for years or decades upon our shelves may speak to us again — like memories, yet more potent for staying as they are in print while it is we who may change in such a way as to pick up brand new messages from battered old volumes.

For example: It's right here. Here I read the portion of *Torah* named the Akedah and in 2025 I saw something I had not seen before in the written narrative. Here was/is a book I had read many times yet, this year, I saw and understood something new in the words. How on Earth? How come I saw something new in these familiar words, bound as they are into books?

And let's take another look, from a new perspective, at another influential book: Jansen's *History of Art*. I toted Jansen around for several semesters during my Junior and Senior years of college, studying Art, cap A. And talk about stupid, or maybe I should just ease up and call my little self of that era 'blunted' — I was thus so blunted in my own intelligence and my own perspective that I did not even notice at that time how there were NO women artists in the entire Jansen index. None. So what now? What do I note now about that book — bound and quite heavy — what I see and intuit so clearly and so, sadly, late in my life is the message that you, the female, have no place in art history. And it is spoken, without words, right here on Earth of that time in my life that you, a woman, have no words. You are to remain silent. And I did. Remain silent. After college graduation with my BA in Art of all things, all I strove to do was to manage to live after being with my mother as she died and to find and keep money-paying jobs — female type jobs — working in a couple of department stores, bra department, and in an art library at Chouinard surrounded by more and more books that never featured women who could paint. Not even good ol' Grandma Moses — nary a mention of women who paint. Then I hit the jackpot for a writer: Advertising. I became an advertising copywriter. TV. Radio. Longform print. Big bucks for a little woman with an unbound tongue.

It's so embarrassing and frustrating and astonishing that I did not have more powers of observation way back then. But the book I carried, still spoke to me. You are nobody. You are not even a ghost studying art, so-called, during your higher, so-called, education.

So that's how on Earth books speak. Jansen is devious. Secretive? Snotty!

Then, in 2025 I discover the complexities of how another book — our book of scripture — speaks to us and I discover, again, how women's tongues are bound. And that all three dominant religions revere the same passages created by love of and belief in, the Divine source for the writing contained in this book.

So now, will I be disinherited of my chosen belief-system pathway? Will I be considered to be too opinionated to be still, validly, a Jewish woman? Part of me will always need to study more, to think more, to engage more with *Torah* than my peers — the born and raised Jewish friends I have. What does

Mary know? She's only a Con-Vert.

This is hard medicine to swallow. Hearing the word, exaggerated, with a sneering tone of what I can only call 'mockery' I am called a CON-vert out there in the many synagogue parking lots I have occupied during studies and classes. Oof. And I have overheard that same diminishing tone of voice when others of my ilk have also spoken up in shul. So here is what I propose:

Since I made a commendable income as an advertising copywriter, I will insert a different descriptor, a punchier headline, into my Jewish self-definition: Volunteer. Yes I like that. Sounds like I am now an active member, who, of her own free will, joined the tribe. Dove right into my own mikvah. Made my pledges to study for the rest of my lifetime. Volunteers often do the scutwork of various organizations – serving at food lines, helping children at road crossings, writing notes to US Senators. Volunteers may not often rise to leadership, but it's not impossible, is it? I also like the free-will feel of the word VOLUNTEER. Nobody made me do this. Nobody threatened me, pushed me. I did the work. Studied. Prepared essays for rabbis. Contemplated. Who does that nowadays – contemplate? Then I walked on my own, right up to, and into, my own mikvah. And, by whomever god may be, I have made good on all my pledges and promises – keenest of which was to study *Torah* and all thinkers Jewish, for the rest of my days.

Done. And doing, still.

And so, no more with this CON-vert stuff. Call me if you must: a Volunteer. I done good. Look at this:

I have written five books with Jewish themes, four novels and a single memoir and I received recognition and accolades in the form of WINNER literary awards on each and every Jewish-themed book I have created. One small disappointment: my work is yet to be featured in Jewish publications. Not for lack of trying. Ah, well. Onward. I have another book in progress. You hold it right now in your hands. We shall see.

And thus I begin to understand more clearly how books speak to us sometimes well beyond the moments when we actually sit down to read them.

Then, if and when I put my fears, my distress, into words, some reader will observe:

"You shouldn't be so sensitive."

"You shouldn't be so sensitive."

How many times and by how many people will I need to hear this admonishment?

And right away I am blamed for one of my traits which I value as one of my most treasured assets — my sensitivity. In a world of insensitivity, of brutality, of triviality, of skimming over important passages in books for example, surface dwellers, unable to probe subtlety or complexity for greater insight. And let's not start in on the sensitivity of eyesight. Vision. When an artist makes art, they see things that perhaps nobody else can see. That's a whole nuther subject.

I may be tut-tutted for having too much of that very quality that I believe qualifies me as a particular species of person. A 'deep' person? Well, that may be framed as a scoffing remark. Deep. Well, la-de-dah! Mary's a brain. Yes. Heard that in school a lot and it was not a compliment. It was kid stuff, scorn. So I laid low a lot during school days.

"Oh, Mary. You are just too sensitive."

You can't win this one, Mary. It's just one word. Sensitive. Yet it contains several meanings. Treasured meanings.

Disputed meanings. The same word: 'sensitive'. Let's take a little diversion and check it out.

To clearly understand what the word 'sensitive' means, let's look it up. Open if you can, and if you cannot do this in actual life because you do not own the complete set of the *Oxford English Dictionary*, well nevermind.

I 'heart' the Oxford English Dictionary

Take my hand from the handiwork of these pages I have written. Take these pages and let's look up the words: *sensitive, sensitivity, sensitiveness* and *sensitizer*. All related yet wonderfully descriptive.

And I quote:

Sensitive . . . Having the function of sensation or sensuous perception . . .

Sensitive plant . . . Possessing a high degree of irritability, causing the leaflets of the bipinnate leaves to fold together at the slightest touch . . . mimosa or sensitive fern . . .

Well, that is not precisely what I am looking for.

As with many dictionary definitions, the reader may select which ones work best to define a certain aspect of any given word. For example these:

With reference to mental feelings: Having quick and acute sensibilities, easily touched to emotions, impressionable, easily wounded by unkindness, occasionally, ready to take offense . . .

Okay. Better. How 'bout this one:

. . . One in whom the sensitive faculty is highly developed . . . Keen susceptibility to outward impressions, delicacy or keenness of feeling developed to an unusually or abnormal degree . . .

Closer. A bit critical with its use of the word 'abnormal'. See, Mary. You are just too sensitive and that may be interpreted as 'abnormal'.

Hmmmm. Let's try another one:

An eloquent exuberance characterizes the style of our author, and a sensitivity of imagination which makes even the minutest phenomenon appear important to one's attention.

I like it!

Then this last:

A person or thing that has a sensitizing effect, one who reacts by being sensitive to stimulus rather than repressing it.

Even better.

This variation of sensitive and sensitizer makes me come out the hero in my tendency to being too sensitive. Take that! All you repressed out there! See. See. I am by some definitions, 'eloquent' and 'exuberant' showing sensitivity of imagination' and I may be all of these but I am NOT repressed. Like so many of the rest of my world.

You see what a help the *Oxford English Dictionary* can be in settling opinions that come fluttering all around us. It's a regular textbook of how to live in a complicated world of words and opinions. Way better than *Psych. One*.

This book – mine, my voice here – is one of those genres of writing labeled: autobiography. Yes? Something written by women. How she does go on and on. How off-topic she gets. How obsessive. Hey, how bitter she sounds. How can we go on to read the rest of what this woman has to say? She's always talking about herself.

Well, er, hence the word 'auto' tagged onto 'biography'. Sheesh.

Well then, don't continue reading this book.

In my anger and frustration, as witnessed just now a few pages back, in my screed, I wish I could have been – from the beginning of my discussion of the Akedah, I wish I had been brave enough to talk more like Katrina. But I had to create a fictional character and I did so in Kat's way of speaking on this Earth. And it was crazily exhilarating for me, woman author of auto-fiction or of autobiography. Using Kat's voice was liberating. And you see here, within this chapter of this book, you can observe some of my own spleen, thus vented, that she, my fictional character of Katrina – the tone of voice Kat let loose in me, your author of this book and look at what it released in me. And perhaps has answered the question:

"What are we going to do now, Mary Carter?"

Now I'm Going to Talk About Gary

He's 84 now. He irons, now.

Last year he took up ironing. We don't use paper napkins. We have a ton of fabric napkins collected over years, well half a century to be precise, napkins from many iterations of our lives. We use them every time we eat. Gary felt it looked sloppy to just fold the napkins after washing. So, now he irons all our fabric napkins, every week after laundering. It's a pile of rumpled napkins. And Gary squeaks open the ironing board, that old ironing board shrieks rather, when he unfolds it and I am now married to a man who irons.

As an opening gambit at table, during dinners with new-ish friends, the question often gets asked:

"How'd you guys meet?"

Harmless enough. Sometimes witty. We've probably all heard many stories of love and falling, thereof, IN. And most of us have a pre-packaged version of the truth that won't overtake an entire dinner conversation and, as it is, we couples-ly dispute one another, a little cranky, about dates forgotten, episodes mis-remembered. It's how couples respond to this seemingly simple question

"It wasn't the forth, honey. No, no. It was the sixth".

We each hope for gentle chuckles and smiling nods all round the dinner table, acknowledging that, well anyway:

"Here we are. Still."

I've been thinking a lot lately about how to address this question. How much to include. What really happened? And how on Earth did you two manage to find each other? All that. And how have you lasted as long as you have?

Almost fifty years. No. A bit more than fifty. Can't do the math.

Ruth Bader Ginsburg was asked to what she attributed her long marriage and her measured response was:

"Sometimes it's important to be just a little bit deaf."

I love that.

He Had Sad Eyes

That's him. Gary W. Priester. Together we are since 1974. I can't even do the math for that. Going into year 52. I think.

Gary was a type that I fell for. Sexy artsy type. Okay. Yes. Turned out he was an advertising art director. Good. Right. Recently divorced. Good. Even better. That works. Owned a little tract house in Palos Verdes. Cute. Nicely illustrated by Gary with wall art in the living room. Okay. Okay. Beard and longish black hair. Yeah. That works. No kidding. Yet, maybe it's evident here in this snapshot — he had sad eyes.

Here's how this works.

When it's all madness and luv and we're both in our thirties, age-wise and a bit wiser in the brain department, you may not fill in all the blanks about the hardest parts of your life thus far. You give one another a brief outline of your life – oh yeah – and then this happened and then that happened and if there's a bad part you just glide over it with the short version of your life's memorandum. Not all that bad. Not all that much to tell. It's as if you need to test this mad fun love affair. Is he to be trusted? Is she? Will this or that past memory of life sound just too, well, too threatening or too weird or too sad for the other one of us to tolerate? Can this mad crazy love take it? Can our mad love withstand news of deep hurt from dim pasts? So we both dance around each other. Leave the hard stuff for later – if there is any such stuff and if there ever is a later – leave it be buried in this fun new love affair. Caution. Don't touch.

So here, too, I follow my pattern of NOT speaking up. Not saying too much. There are blank silences at times, during our first couple of years. Times when I did not delve too much into my stories. After just a few months 'together' as a defined couple, Gary asked me to move in with him. Perversely, I was not just thrilled at the idea. I shut down. He was hurt and shocked. But I just shut down. Got real quiet. I remember curling up on my bed in my nice tidy little apartment and feeling very threatened. Gary tried to talk with me. He drove across town to talk in person. It took me a long long while to finally say:

"You don't understand. In this apartment I have a stove, a

refrigerator, a sofa and a record-player and I bought them all with my own money. From mediocre jobs I survived by, after my divorce. From my own brand new credit cards that I had had to earn after having to cut up my old ones, with my former married name, in front of our divorce attorneys — cards I had to work to get, and I did work hard at boring jobs — to obtain those credit cards. Everything in this little apartment is here by my own efforts. My survival. What would happen if I moved into your house and we broke up? Would I get my 'stuff' back? My life?"

Well, Gary did manage a humorous comment:

"I could certainly get you a better stereo than that awful record-player here."

I have a stove, refrigerator, a sofa, and a record player and I bought them with my own money.

So you won't believe it: We typed up an agreement, a document on paper, listing my major possessions. Plus a state-of-the-art stereo for whatever era we might be parting in. And assuring that Gary would replace all items on the list. Sofa, refrigerator, stove, record-player. And I made us both sign it. And I placed it in my safe deposit box. There. Well, then: Here we are. Still.

Well, I guess it's turned out okay. And here I am on a state-of-the-art computer for my sound system. I am not ungrateful. Simply cautious.

Well, it's obvious that throughout this book, throughout my narrative from my perspective, I am now telling it like it is. Some of which causes me very great nervous anxiety. I still do not know if I should be writing about some of these things. For example:

Gary had graduated from Art Center. I had sent for their catalog when I was in high school. Big square book with a huge orange circle on the cover. I had pleaded with my mother to go there instead of university. She was intransigent. NO. You need a BA from a real university to fall back on. She and I had bitter and continuing fights over her notions about college. Yet, here was Gary. He turned out okay. But she was long dead by then. I couldn't even say: 'told you so'.

Gary by Gary

It would be even more problematic, presumptuous actually, to reveal some of Gary's most hurtful hurts. It would not feel right for me to dive into his most cherished and guarded memories in order to tell more about him with his sad eyes.

But to fill in a morsel of Gary's backstory, here is an excerpt from a book of short stories that Gary himself wrote and published. A WINNER in the 2023 New Mexico-Arizona Book Awards for Short Fiction. Gary's book *Ernest's New Watch* may include portions of his 'real life' in the words of one of its chapters. The character in the story is six-and-a half years old and his name is David. His mother's name in this story is Adrienne. Here is an excerpt from *Ernest's New Watch:*

> *"So, David was deeply confused when one day, out of the blue, Adrienne announced to him that he was getting a new father. David was speechless. It was just more than his young mind could fathom.*
>
> *When he saw his real father that weekend for his monthly visit, David casually bragged to his father . . . that he was getting a new father. The look of shock, mixed with sadness, mixed with anger, showed on his father's face. . . . His father was at a loss for words. Finally he composed himself and said, "Davie, I am your father. And I love you very, very, much." . . . Tears started welling up in young David's eyes, and he stammered, "N-n-no. I d-d-don't understand." And he burst into tears. . . . Around this time David began to stutter."*

When it was revealed in current journalism that President Biden had been a stutterer and that he battled to this present day how to work around his own linguistic thicket, I saw at once the familiarities between him and Gary in their spoken words. And when politics and its practitioners took up stuttering as a fault, as a target for chiding and poking fun, I bristled as hard as if it were my very own Gary who was being hurt.

What a disgusting path to take through the weeds of another person's daily speaking life. What an era we inhabit where cruelty in spoken words is viewed as machismo. Well ya know what buster? You bullies who use mockery with jabs and har-de-har-har, T'aint funny McGee. You bullies are fat and mindless and vicious and you and your malarky both stink. And I might add, Fuck you you fucking fuckers.

Politics and its practitioners aimed at stuttering as a fault, as a target for chiding and mockery.

In Sickness and In Health

We said those words in 1976. Blithely. Maybe. Yet we had both had early ill-advised first marriages. Same words. But, well, not quite. And the words remain for generations of brides and bridegrooms. Without much questioning, regardless of religious beliefs. Well, of course, there are the modern couples who remove those words or others from the traditional, and now-threadbare, vows. We weren't one of those. We were a couple immersed in the tides of mad love and daily duties. Both of us employed and plenty busy in the field of advertising. Gary, as an art director. Me, as a copywriter. Parting early in the day to tackle the Harbor Freeway. Speeding home — as if, on that freeway — after work and well after dark, headlines popping up along the way out to where we had our home in Rancho Palos Verdes.

If there was any single vow that would weigh in harshest, this one — In sickness and in health — would step up and demand patient fearful witness and violent painful evidence.

I have thought a lot about how, or whether even, to speak about my illness. It always seems voyeuristic to read passages in written narratives when the author chooses to share horrific details of illness. Why? I always ask. Why tell the reader all these gory details? I have come to believe that it's some kind of showing off on an author's part to see who can provide the most stomach-turning verbal descriptions of deathly illness. See. See what a talented wordsmith I am. Same with sex scenes. Why? Why do so very many authors flaunt their cleverness by describing the thrusts of body parts and the shooting of liquids within scenes of passion?

So I, on the one hand, want to demonstrate Gary's steadfast and even his deeply confused and frightened loyalty to our vows of 'in sickness and in health'. Gary had been my husband for about twenty years when the worst of it struck me.

I had been ill since I was thirteen. Various violent cramps and wildly off-calendar events. My mother assured me that I would outgrow these things and that was that. No doctor visits. Just optimism that I would outlive my maladies.

Leaping ahead to my twenties: with the availability of birth control pills, my first very own doctor assured me that much of my years of agony would disappear when I started on those pills. And he was quite right. And so I entered my young adult years with regular relief from horrible pain. I took those miracle pills for about 20 years.

Then, with the wisdom of brand new theories of drugs and women's health, another doctor of mine insisted that I had to give the pills a break. That 'they' — whomever they were — had determined that women should not take the pills for the rest of their lives. So. I quit. Cold. I was just shy of forty.

And that is when my condition upped its ante on my well-being. I became subject to violent attacks. If I were to describe them herein, you, dear reader, would shudder and say:

"No kidding. Those were violent attacks."

Lying on our dressing room floor, right next to the toilet, me in agony, Gary would come over and try to comfort me and to give me a blanket or to help me, god knew how. He was shaking with fear and frightened by the violence of my attacks. I lay on the floor suffering waves of rhythmic spasms of excruciating pain and nausea. And Gary was so frightened. But he never left my side.

Skipping backwards, I sought help from several doctors. And it was this wisdom:

"Well, Mary. You need to buck up. Try a little Midol. Aspirin. You'll be just fine."

No.

It got worse.

There was the medical proviso of that era that I could not seek surgery to end this horror until I reached age forty. When that finally came, I found my surgeon, and made my appointment. You'll like this part: in order to get this surgery, I had to sign a document that stated that I understood that the procedure would be permanent. And this: I had to go to the doctor's office and view a film on how babies were made. The same film we girls all had to view around the sixth grade. It was even a very old jittery film strung into a humming film projector in a dim room. It was so outrageous, I started to fume — inwardly, mind you. And I had to sign another document that said I had understood the film.

I said to myself:

"Well, old girl. Just sign this stupid, insulting, document. And let's get out of here. And let's get this over with."

But the best part is this, if 'best' isn't too grim:

My surgeon strides up to my hospital bed after the operation. She had on her folded arm a clipboard with my papers. She had the results of the pathology report of my removed organs. Nothing was digital back then when I was forty. She began to give me the deets:

"Well, it wasn't cancer, you'll be glad to know. The examination of your organs showed you may have only ovulated five or six times in your entire lifetime up to now. And you had the following two conditions. She named them. You could have died, ya know?"

Not nice and fuzzy, this surgeon. Her tone of voice reciting this to me was peevish and cranky, like an impatient adult speaking to a difficult child. As if I were somehow to blame for my condition.

My response:

"I've been telling that to doctors, all along, ya know. When can I get out of here?"

"Well, we need to see that you are able to relieve yourself after the surgery."

"I'm on it."

Life saving procedure? My doctor's tone of voice was pissed, bothered, just this side of angry at me. As if I had been somehow to blame for my very messed up anatomy. Appropriate words: 'Fucked up' come to mind. Really. It was way worse.

Gary and I spoke right after I came to. I told him about the doctor's feedback. We were both relieved. I in particular, as I relieved myself in that hospital, then walked out in less than 24 hours after my surgery.

Subsequently I have discovered, talking with my current family doctor, that recent medical training includes more and vastly improved ways of dealing with women who are experiencing the two conditions that I had had. He was somewhat apologetic, chagrinned I sensed, that I had had to endure doctors' arrogance and cruelty and ignorance during that era on top of a very cruel and excruciatingly painful condition, a potentially life-threatening illness. But importantly? Gary was with me throughout the worst of it all. And he is with me now in 2025. Still.

Backwards On We Go

When I wrote the following words in the last chapter:

He was somewhat apologetic, chagrinned I sensed, that I had had to endure doctors' arrogance and cruelty and ignorance during that era on top of a very cruel and excruciatingly painful condition, a potentially life-threatening illness.

Well here we are again. Women. Silenced. And this time it's killer silence. Dangerous. You can die from your symptoms. You can be ignored. You can be shoved to one side in a hospital corridor, doctors trembling in fear of arrest. Try obtaining even a seemingly innocuous D&C and you or your doctor, both, can both be arrested. Even accused of murder. It's 2025. The law is no longer favorable to women. Better keep your legs tightly crossed and your mouth tightly shut.

I ignored or failed to or have been afraid to tackle this subject but I am going to tell it like it is now. Pregnant women who suffer life-threatening complications to their bearing of children are in serious danger of bleeding to death long before it is 'decided' by doctors and/or the new law, whether or not to interfere in any pregnancy with surgery. There are many painful and life-threatening situations that may develop in pregnancy, that can kill a mother and/or her infant. And, as I experienced, there are several other life-threatening conditions that some percentage of non-pregnant woman may experience as well. Several, many, diagnosed or undiagnosed conditions related to being a woman, can kill. And do.

First a bit of history:

For all of you educated male people out there in positions of power you need to know this: women have for centuries, have always — and in all ways — ended their own pregnancies when driven to doing so by dire circumstances. Circumstances, I want to emphasize, assisted in major part by males. Pregnancy requires two fertile people — one female, one male. Did'ya know that? In case it's no longer legal to differentiate males and females, I just wanted to make sure we're all on the same page about how pregnancies occur. Yet the hatred and vituperation is always and in all ways, heaped upon the woman who takes her womb into her own hands. Other than passing and remaking laws to support the anonymity of males, men have done nothing — no thing — to comfort and assist women in their most desperate circumstances. You cannot turn to your male partner, or male assailant, if he has already turned on you. Yet if you speak of it to family, friends so-called, newspapers, or the courts you will be accused of 'asking for it'. You will be crucified on the sharp pointed edges of the law and opinion. Yet, throughout human history, there have always been other women to help, assist, advise, protect, or to hide women – some of them their own daughters – to find a way to help or assist pregnant or non-pregnant girls and women – including with terminating a pregnancy.

Here's a true story from my own mother on this topic. She of course warned me about unplanned pregnancies. BUT once I was of high school age she stressed:

"Please do not be afraid to come to me if you are pregnant and don't know what to do. Do not be afraid of coming to me. I will help you no matter what. If you decide to end the pregnancy, I will take you to Sweden or Japan for an abortion. But you know what Mary? If you decide to keep the child, I will help you raise him and he will be the best kid on the block."

She said these things more than once during my teen years. Repeating her promise to help me no matter what, so that I'd remember her words. And I have.

The dawn shone briefly upon securing safe passage and female authority when *Roe v. Wade* came into law. I remember it well. Driving home from work in my dusty little tan VW, listening to the local Rock n' Roll radio station, the recording was halted and the announcer stated that it was now legal for women to obtain abortions. I pulled my car over to the curb, shifted into neutral and sobbed against the steering wheel. Finally. At last. Some relief from fear, from back rooms, from men pretending to be gynecologists, from poverty, from sickness, from death. Oh yes. You better cry now Mary Carter — that's what you're going to have to do now. But you know what? Just a few months ago, after fifty years of surcease, I heard on another car radio the backwards version of *Roe v. Wade* — the law withdrawn by the wise men of the court's highest ranking males. And same same same, now all over again, back to the good-old bad-old days. But worse, way worse, now in this 21st Century.

Welcome women to the binding of your tongues.

Without *Roe* you will have no say about how your body — its most private and precious parts — how your body will be treated, or *not* treated, by modern, so-called, medicine. If left to bleed out from a disaster of pregnancy, you may well end like Sarah:

"And Sarah's life was a hundred and twenty-seven years, the years of Sarah's life."

Except it will be your name, yours, whose life may have been well under thirty years, mere, the years of your life. Think about it. Without *Roe* you have no life of your own. You have no tongue to speak about what is life and what is death.

You will have no say. Your tongue will be bound. Choke on that dear and beloved women, suffering from being constructed as women.

My Offspring

But do not conclude that Gary and I are disappointed in our singularity as a childless couple. We are not.

It was potentially a life-threatening illness and it turned out to threaten the very life of any possibility for my giving birth to a human offspring.

As yet another example of my recurrent silences, I wonder, now, how it is that I had never had an urge to have a child. And have never been disappointed in my lack. Never. But now that I have passed so many sunrises, sunsets, I wonder if my body or some singular fold within my brain had been communicating to me its wishes or opinions for my future somehow based upon internal knowledge about my body's missing segments. The dysfunctional parts. That, not having been formed correctly, missing some anatomical elements, that some form of silent communication, non verbal, had prepared me for the discovery that, as my chilly surgeon informed me:

"You could never have conceived."

I wonder. Is this how I have remained without regrets as to not bearing kin, and remaining childless? As if we — my poorly constructed anatomy along with my mind and soul, or perhaps my subconscious, had guided me to contentment in other paths of birthing — as an artist, as a writer.

My body, mind, and soul are okay with this as am I, along with them in my life choices. You might perceive this to be rationalization — well, maybe it is — yet I do not feel, and never have felt, traumatized by my inadequacy.

The good part is this — I have given birth to many offspring — Goose Girls, Chicken Lady, Sarah Steinway, Tova Goodman, Mrs. Annette Zinn along with a huge contingent of stretched canvasses that burst out of our garage and insist upon eyes to view them. Strolling through an old portfolio of drawings I made immediately after my wakening from my ten year fugue, all dated 1979, I have to brag:

"Not bad, old girl. These drawings are damn good, old girl!"

Gary, A Character With Character

Gary was drafted during Vietnam. And by coincidence, for his first job after college graduation from Art Center, he was offered a position as an art director at Grey Advertising in Detroit. When he received the job offer, shortly after graduation day, he told Grey management that he was now subject to being drafted immediately. They said, okay, they would keep him on staff for as long as possible. Gary moved to Detroit for the job. He would be there for a few months. Then his draft number was up. It was known that some young draftees fled to Canada from Detroit and while Gary knew about this, he did not do that. He simply showed up for his military induction and said later:

"I would just see how it went."

Through a series of coincidences he was first placed in the Corps of Engineers to make maps and he figured he would be sent to Vietnam, but would work in a trailer rather than on the field of battle. In a peculiar turn of events, Gary was sent to South Korea. He did maps there for the rest of his service. Mostly these were maps to officer's homes for parties.

Later, much later, in another peculiar event, and as it turns out a quite magical one, something happened that would change Gary's life.

He and I met at a party and, eyes across the room, I saw that he had sad eyes. The first time he brought me to his home, I sat on the sofa with my glass of wine and up popped KP — Kitty Priester. She made my lap her sofa, turned around, curled her paws in kitty comfort posture and started purring.

"What a friendly kitty."

And I leaned down and kissed her forehead.

Later, and for years later, Gary tells me that KP had never sat on any girl's lap that he had ever brought home. And, in fact, that she would race out her kitty door and never return whenever he brought a girl home. But she came right up to me and made a lap and she and I became instant friends. Kitty

Priester. She saw what and who she approved of and we were friends ever after.

Decision made. Gary knew I was The One. Kitty Priester was in the lead on that most important decision.

The cousins insinuated that I had glommed onto Gary for his money.

I knew if they confronted me, cowards that they were, I doubted that they would say this to my face, but I had an answer, just in case.

"Not money. Sex."

But back to Gary's being a Character with Character. He can be surprising.

Gary's Aunt Bea

Gary used always to remind me that the definition of a genius is a boy with a Jewish Grandmother. When he and I were getting acquainted, I quipped:

"Funny kind of Jew. You don't do anything Jewish."

And he shot back:

"Well you know, we are Beverly Hills Jews. Norah Ephron, the author, has dubbed us: 'Christmas tree Jews."

I could observe Gary's family resemblance every time we visited Aunt Bea in LA or when we had her up to Marin County to visit us for a few days.

It is interesting to note that Bea had a short but persistent list of grumbles in her life. One was a mother-in-law she did not like. No surprise there. And another was an historic gripe about something her husband, Uncle Martin, had done, many years ago. Or I should amend, what he did not do.

When Bea and he were middle aged, he decided to purchase places for the family in the Jewish Cemetery. He reserved and purchased three spots in the marble wall of crypts. One for his sister — Gary's mother. One for his mother — Gary's grandmother. And one for himself. He had not purchased one for Aunt Bea — his wife.

She was hurt. Furious. Hurt more and more. Then she took action. She went right over to the Jewish Cemetery and purchased the marble crypt right above her husband's spot.

"That way, at least I'll be buried face down and be right on top of him."

But that act did not assuage her hurt and anger.

Thus, every time we got together with Bea, just the three of us, she would return to her, by this time, familiar beef. Decades had passed and her husband had already been placed in his spot and she was still stewing about it.

So during one such session, the three of us seated under our umbrella on a bright sunny morning, in she went again. Grumbling and angry and hurt and on and on and on. We had heard it all many times by now. Maybe on this occasion it was near to the funeral for her husband and so we all had to walk by the spot for the 'placement'. But on she went, reviewing her hurt and anger at this, monumental, mistake of Uncle Martin's.

But finally Gary interrupted:

"Move Grandma."

Bea's eyes lit up. There was sort of a giggle in her voice.

"Move Grandma. Put her in the mausoleum spot right above Uncle Martin. Which would leave the one next to him empty. For you, Bea. Move Grandma."

"Can I do that?"

The idea was warming.

"You can do whatever you want to, Bea. He's dead. You're still alive. Just do it. Move Grandma."

"But, but how can I do that?"

"You can do whatever you damn-well please. You certainly can afford it. You've got the money. Just move Grandma."

Gary was indeed, a character with character.

And so, after Aunt Bea's memorial service and they wheeled her casket out to the mausoleum and we saw the open crypt next to Uncle Martin, ready for the 'placement', Gary whispered to me:

"Move Grandma."

Then again, there was this side to Aunt Bea: She was generous in her reasons for her generosity.

As a very well off woman living in Beverly Hills, she was constantly being sought out by many charities. She would listen patiently to many pitches in her own home, over tea or coffee. One such, a group of three leaders from the YMCA, went through their own presentation, complete with photos of the old van and photo of a proposed new van. Bea paid quiet attention. Looking at the photo of the brand new model, she asked:

"How much is this one?"

They stated the total amount.

"Excuse me for a moment. I will be right back."

She went upstairs to her desk, wrote a check and returned. Handing it to them, with no further words, the committee saw that it was a check for the entire price of the new van.

Then this:

On another occasion, Bea was approached by leaders of what would be a new wing for a homeless women's shelter. Bea asked if she could see the actual building and the proposed plans. They drove her across town to Venice and took her on a tour of the facilities. Bea told me it hit her very hard. She wrote a generous check and I asked her:

"What moved you to decide on that amount for your donation?"

And she simply replied and repeated:

"There but for fortune go I. I could have ended up there.

However, there, but for fortune, could have gone I."

I believe that some portion of Gary's character took root in living near a family member like Aunt Bea.

Ungrateful Wretch

So I have always thought that I have been gracious and modest about my appearance. Since the moment at the orthodontist's waiting room, with its aquarium illuminated by bright green lightbulbs, I grinned into the mirror behind the swishing fishes and thought for the first time ever:

"I'm pretty."

I was surprised and pleased — to put it mildly — by my new looks. For two years this office, with two cheery and dedicated orthodontists twisting and pulling and shoving metal tools and parts excruciatingly at my teeth, every other week, between my eleventh and thirteenth years — they forced my mouth away from my former buck-toothed goofy English grin. I was now, finally, even-toothed, smooth of jaw and, well, pretty. This was mind-bending, nearly hallucinogenic, news to my as yet undeveloped pre-teenage mind.

And I fell for it.

Started reading *Seventeen* and taking much to heart beauty tips and before and after pictures of already pretty girls and looking at my new self with a hand-held mirror — front, sides, back and figuring out how to "do" my hair to enhance the whole effect of this new me.

Ironically, and somewhat predictably, one of my first real jobs was working on *Seventeen* in their West Coast Offices on Wilshire Blvd. Copywriter, captions. Go-to girl: combs, brushes and makeup for models. Toter of hip clothes. Pinner of crooked hems. I got business cards that touted me as West Coast Fashion Editor. Great title. Paid shit. But I could borrow any of the clothes left over after our fashion shoots. Hats. Miniskirts. Only problem was, I had by then taken my first husband's name so I couldn't gloat much with former college pals when my name appeared on the masthead. See Mary Hollyfield. That's me. Or was. Noting the year 1971, that was the year of my divorce.

Sadly, the West Coast Editor was THE worst supervising BOSS that I would ever work with. She would routinely toss my pages at me and they would flutter onto her lime green carpeting and she'd yell:

"Do Something!!"

And, seeking input, I'd ask what it needed and she'd yell:

"I don't know. You're the writer. JUST. DO. SOMETHING."

What I learned about copywriting from working on *Seventeen* was just one thing and here's how it went:

I was taken aside by the ad manager for west coast *Seventeen*, for a little talk behind closed doors. He had in his hand my monthly Expense Report — lunches with clients and suchall, gas to and from fashion shoots at, say, the beach and back to Wilshire — and this man, suited and tied, was not pleased. He said my Expenses put to shame his expenses. And he rattled off things like my $5.00 gas tab, and $24.50 for lunch. He said his Expenses were considerably more and that my Expense Report put to question HIS Expense Report. So to solve this discrepancy, what I was to do with my future reports was to

INCREASE them exponentially. Add wine to the lunches. I didn't do wine at lunch. Nevermind. Put it in your Expense Report. Your expenses must come to at least more than $100. For each one. Well, well. He sure told me. My first lesson in corporate accounting.

By the way — how'd I get such a glam job, with its glam title, as writing on *Seventeen?*

Well, I had a short-term job on *California Men's Stylist Magazine* writing snarky and hip fashion reviews of new clothing lines and retail stores for men. I have always been the mistress of snark and the editor of *Seventeen* had been following my weekly columns for a while. When *Men's Stylist* went belly up, she hired me, then and there. No interviews.

There was a hiatus to my writing career. Divorce. Change back to my 'maiden' name. Working for a few months in a snazzy San Francisco store. Moving back to LA. Meeting Gary — more to follow on this part.

Later I managed to become an advertising copywriter on real consumer accounts like writing TV, print, and radio copy for clients that included: Taco Bell, Sea World, Bank of America, Home Savings, MPS Chunks Dog Food, and Little Friskies cat food. I gotta boast. Right? I ultimately worked as an advertising copywriter at three of the biggest advertising agencies on Wilshire Blvd — Foote, Cone & Belding Honig Cooper & Harrington (say that in just one breath), as well as Erwin Wasey, and then onto the biggest of the big-timers on Wilshire, Grey Advertising, where I was hired by Grey's First Woman Vice President Hooray, Hooray. Ah, those were the days. She turned out to be the best copy supervisor I ever worked with or for. And that job paid real money. At last. And what did I learn about advertising copywriting from Grey? Drink wine at lunch. Take two hours. For lunch. Come in the rear door of the agency after lunch. Resume wine around 4:15 in the Downstairs Conference Room — pseudonymously named by us copywriters. All the secretaries knew where to find us if some suit came round needing a speedy headline for this or that.

I would muse to myself, "... at least nobody died."

So I took it all in as a pretty girl, youngish woman (I was still under forty during those stints) and I believed that I was both pretty and talented. Smart, too, as if anybody cared. In advertising, per our remit as copywriters, smart was not a major asset for a copywriter. Much more appreciated was our ability to instantly dash out headlines and body copy in severe RUSH circumstances. All the rest of my job consisted of enduring marketing meetings in rooms full of suited management-types and taking in all that blather, making notes even, about consumer preferences and it was simply all inuendo, all the time, 'cause the conference table was filled with all those powerful men in dark suits that their mothers had purchased for them as soon as they graduated with their SCMBA's. And the fury at this or that 'stat' or rewriting target massaging for the umpteenth time. Cleaning up the administrative language for big client meetups. The manipulative puffery coming at me from all around that huge Mahogony table.

"Well . . ."

I would muse to myself,

". . . at least nobody died."

Well, at least those meetings and that work continues to pay me to write the kind of book that you are now holding in your hands, right here, right now, today. My IRA account, assembled from advertising copywriting positions from long ago, still chugs along, investing back to me its modest earnings.

But I was talking about pretty.

I had been such a sucker for my good fortune. It was that early '50s orthodontia that changed the direction of who I would become in later life. Funnily enough, lately, my dentist commented that I must have had orthodontia done during the fifties.

"How do you know?", I asked.

"We now have a very different way of working with buck teeth and such. I can see that you had at least two of your 'big' teeth removed from the very back of your upper jaw to make room for pushing the top teeth painfully back into that vacated space. And that you are missing a middle tooth between your canines on the bottom and that you were missing at least one or perhaps both of your upper wisdom teeth. We don't do it like that any more. I bet it was pretty painful for you."

No kidding.

Back in those days, becoming pretty took a team, tools, time, pain. But then there it was. My greenish fishtank smile. I'm pretty.

Keeping Secrets

So here's another question: How on Earth do we talk to our parents? How on Earth do they talk to us? How do we learn how and when NOT to talk to our parents? How exactly does this work? I mean, here I am, eighty-ish and I'm still stewing over something my mother said and then what I said and then that thing she shouted and then I shouted back. All this when I was a lippy teenager. Not a fond memory, but persistent. And what I always end up thinking about it is how on Earth I learned NOT to talk to my mother. Not to shout. So there's some sort of premium I have in my memory about how we learn to stay mum around our mums.

I'm not going to switch gears to make this book a deeply researched study of: How on Earth do we talk with or to our parents?

To prune and focus this topic I have decided to use my own narrow range as an only child born before there were freeways in the San Fernando Valley. Educated at all brand new schools — from elementary school, to junior high school, all the way to high school — the schools of my generation were all tossed together during our summers off.

First each June there was freshly poured blacktop. Then square stucco structures, called 'temps,' were plunked down upon the reeking tar. Jaunty yellow, hastily painted, handball borderlines appeared, and voila, presto, there was next semester's school. I attended two temps for my sixth semester, two temps I attended for Junior high, and one double session for eighth grade, shared with a high school campus while they built our brand new junior high school which I attended for only one year during my final year before high school. I then joined the very first class to attend our brandy-brand new high school, William Howard Taft High School in Woodland Hills. So there I was, again, in amongst a lot of kids I did not know.

The result of these many ad-hoc schools was that my classmates often were placed into different school districts and more often than not, my group of classmates changed as many times as my schools did. There was little continuity to my friends from year to year. The result? I learned by a kind of self-protective osmosis, how to survive in unfamiliar groups of age-cohort classmates. Well, that's not a bad skillset for later in life. And what I learned very quickly and more than adequately, was how to manage class bullies or creeps and how, most importantly, how to glide past those types, keeping to myself, almost anonymous, without harm to myself, and without bringing too much attention my way. I sometimes wonder whatever became of Billy, or Neal or that other guy, what's-his-name.

Oh, and through it all – or maybe because of all the changes from year to year in my schools – I learned for the first time what I should NOT tell my mother. How on Earth do we talk to our parents? And how do we learn that particular skill – keeping mum with Mum, NOT telling all?

Let's see? It was summer before seventh grade – another new school district – another new school. But along with learning about bullies, I also learned about girls who were not altogether innocents. I had a couple of girl friends – they invited me to come see their fort – a bunch of lumber stacked this way and that on an empty lot. I asked my mother if that was okay and she loved the idea. Those two girls were best students in that season's classes. She was thrilled in fact. Great influence for me.

Well, so, of course we clambered under an old grubby canvas doorway into the fort and no sooner inside, they offered me a cigarette. Well, sure. Sophisticated little phony, I accepted. I let them light up for me. Puffed, didn't inhale. And there I was. Holding a secret from my mother. Holding the object of NOT telling her about something. Now then, I was not going to become a liar. I simply decided to just NOT talk about the cigarettes to my mother. Simple. Simply edit them out of my jolly mother-chatter when she came to pick me up from my 'great influencers' that afternoon from their fort.

Now, remember that I discovered, when I turned fifty and then again, when I was about to turn eighty, as I read my mother's wartime letters, that my mother had stories she had not ever told me. In fact, what I discovered back then was that it is probably ALL mothers who likely have stories they have never told their daughters. Likewise for their daughters. Here's a snippet of not telling and so too an example of not listening between mothers and daughters.

Once when I was about fifteen, when my father got home from work, my mother led him into their bedroom and what followed was her crying and some yelling. My mother was never a crier. Never a yeller. I could not make out what they were saying. But I hastened into the living room and turned the TV up, way loud, so that I could not hear them. When the episode was over and the bedroom door opened there was no further discussion. No further tears. I will never know what went on that day. But I did not want to hear it. So how do we learn how to keep secrets from our parents? How on Earth do we learn NOT to talk? And how NOT to listen?

Here's another anecdote that oddly references smoking, coincidentally:

Skipping on to my senior year in college, I am in the car and my mother is driving us off to Robinson's to do a bit of Spring shopping before my last weeks in college before graduation. My mother looks pensive. Then she says she has read several newspaper articles about college students smoking Mara-Wanna. She over pronounces the words, calling it Mara Wanna.

"Have you heard of any kids at your school who smoke Mara Wanna?"

"Uh-huh."

"Do you know of anybody who smokes Mara Wanna?"

"Uh-huh."

"Do you have any friends who smoke Mara Wanna?"

"Uh-huh."

This was getting too close for comfort. As I have said, I was not a liar. But her next question hung there. What could I say?

What could I NOT say. How could I get around it? Not even talk about it?

I looked out the passenger side window as we swung into Robinson's parking lot.

"Oh, there's a good place. Let's go shopping!"

She never asked me her last question about Mara Wanna.

And so, through care and stealth, and perhaps from a variety of tacit agreement, unspoken, I learned how NOT to talk to my mother about certain things. And she gave me the latitude to avoid saying anything to her. As she parked the car in Robinson's parking lot, I could feel her mind ticking away. Should I? Or not? I was never to know. She never asked. I never lied. And there we were. How on Earth do we speak to our parents? How did I learn to stay mum around my Mum? 'Tis a mystery.

Then there is this cherished memory about what and when and how to use swear words:

Playing with our neighbor and his dog Rex, spinning Rex round and round at the end of a ragged old rug, I shouted gleefully and loud, "You Bastard!"

Well that set off my mother from the kitchen.

"Mary! You get in here right now."

And in the kitchen my mother sat me down on the stool next to the window and lectured me about how it was just not okay to use swear words. And she went on and on and on as was her method when upset with me: she had reasons, logic, examples, and on and on and on. Finishing her diatribe, she asked:

"And where on Earth, I ask you Mary, WHERE on Earth did you learn to talk like that?"

"Well, Mama, Grandma calls everybody a bastard."

WHERE on Earth did you learn to talk like that?

My mother burst out laughing, really hard. Spluttering, giggling, laughing again.

"Well my mother. . . She says what she wants. But, you Mary. You should never use the word again."

Lesson learned: don't say Bastard around my mother, at least not within her earshot.

But listen to this: my grandmother had been a working woman, both in her youth near the turn of the Century and also in her later years. She was a Linotype operator on a newspaper for a long time while she was single. In her 'old' age — more than sixty — she crossed some union strike lines at one LA newspaper to keep the linotypes up and running. Not sure what her political views could have been. Probably it was simply her way to refer to strikers, and most likely to management as well, as 'bastards'.

* * *

Here are some pictures of the formidable machines she could control:

Note the long hemlines in all the pix. These snapshots are of my grandmother at work in the linotype room of a newspaper, before the turn of the 20th Century.

In those days there were young men who assisted the linotype operators, but those women operators solidly outranked those young assistants. And, undoubtedly, some of those 'bastards' were her first contributors to my grandmother's harsh tongue. What a guilty pleasure it is to imagine how that went. And what a delicious treat to learn that nobody bound up my grandmother's tongue. Not anybody. Anyhow.

A Woman in Your Corner

(I have changed some names for privacy)

In 1978 there was to be a huge party to celebrate the first woman who rose to the stature, and title, of Vice President at Grey Advertising in Los Angeles. Times had changed. Everybody up and down Wilshire Boulevard was abuzz about the big bash to celebrate her rise to, not quite to the corner office, but near enough, for a female. Every creative department — copywriters, art directors, TV producers, print production managers, plus a certain skeptical contingent of Creative Directors, Capital C, Capital D, who may have felt skeptical but knew, full and well, which sides their bread was buttered on. A woman! Vice President? Are you kidding? Life being short in the ad biz, better show up at the big bash, say your bit, mention your television commercial reel. Hug, hug. Kiss, kiss. Who knows. Maybe someday it'll be **you** sitting in HER office with your portfolio.

The big do was just a couple of blocks down Wilshire from my office atop the Travelers Building and just across the street from the Equitable Building where the new Vice President was to preside, safely to occupy the sixth floor which the man in the corner office thought would be safer in a fire rather than higher floors and you could always flee down the stairs, just in case of emergency. These kinds of executive decisions were de rigueur coming from corner offices in those days.

This party was scheduled for 6:00 PM in the largest party room of the Ambassador Hotel which was just across the street from the Equitable Building. And it was predicted that the entire advertising community would attend and all fit into that huge venue. Champagne, free. Food, optional.

A pal of mine, Joel, had invited me. You can't miss this. And me, thrilled to be invited, me the budding new-hire copy maven for Sea World and Home Savings, I was very keen indeed to attend this of all historic parties. You'll never forget it, Joel assured me.

We arrived around 7:00-ish and the room was already jammed. You could hear the regurgitations of resumes, recent awards, and all the expected blather of self-regard typical of our industry's copywriting talent. Also in boisterous usage were all the copywriters in the room playing clever word tricks with things like 'man-power' changing it to 'person-power' now that these times had changed. Har, har, har, har. Clever, yes?

And there she sat.

Out there in the center of the room at her own round table surrounded by all her busy sycophants.

I want to be her when I grow up.

She was small. Very slender in a slim flower printed silk thingy. A redhead with unruly locks artfully shoved this way and that way. In one hand a cigarette. In her other hand, a martini. She may have laughed but it looked more like whatever was supposed to be funny was just not that funny. Just a tiny bit scornful, her chuckle. A bit bitter. Ironic I tell you, she munched on a 'see I told you so' expression along the edges of her mouth, engaged as it was in her so-called smile.

Matti Maloney.

I nudged Joel and said: "I want to be her when I grow up."

A few years later Matti would be my Creative Group Head – Taco Bell and Bank of America. I had graduated. Got a two panel window looking west, my own desk and a door. Matti was a great boss. Outstanding, always completely loyal to her ratty team of us writers. At the first hint of an argument from management, she'd grab her cigarette, race down the carpeted hallways to the account executives' suite, and 'tear him a new asshole' in stout and loyal defense of our headlines. Tastes Great.

But the weird thing about that celebratory party at the Ambassador Hotel is this: not a single art director or copywriter at that bash ever even mentioned that that had been the room where Bobby Kennedy's assailant lurked. And just through those doors was the kitchen where Kennedy was killed. That had only been ten years ago. And it was, and still is, in all the news reports of that tragedy. And not one of us very clever professionals even mentioned it. And, as a witness, I, too had neither thought nor said a word about it. Sad. Really. Too sad. Bunch of glib talkers and not a word said about that.

The Hard Part: What's the Point?

Returning to those several dinner tables whereat I have been asked this question:

"So, do you write about your own life in your novels?"

As if to denigrate the work – and yes there is some work involved in the act of writing novels – as if to simplify, or even to take for granted, the development of fictional characters, fictional narratives, denouement, and resolution. Well, that's just kid's stuff. Small stuff. Grammar and all that. Right? And all the eminent, presumed, malc authors conquered those things easily within their deep attentions to war and politics. The big stuff. And if those men had personal experience of those things – being a soldier on the field of battle for example – for authors on your college syllabus were able to rise above personal feelings and experiences and to make their fictional accounts **Important** in the pantheon of human thought and observations. Big stuff you see. For each and every one of those men in those syllabi, their fiction works were considered to be Big Stuff.

Well, so moving on. Not to harp as Hannah-Naomi said.

There is something very difficult, if not impossible, for me to get around in creating this albeit non-fiction account of episodes and memories of my life. And it is this:

The inculcation of my specific time and duration upon this Earth enters into my tangled hodge-podge of thoughts. Fear. Frustration. Ignorance. Over-protection. There is an overwhelming inculcation of all past culture on my development as a woman writer and artist who is about to turn eighty. There is no ignoring the fact that I was born into a nice clean moderately fortunate small life in a generally safe space on this Earth. Yet with 'modern' communication vehicles — broadcast news, internet influencers, opinions, opinions, and images, images, videos, texts from friends, even, and as the years proceed, I am brought closer and closer to people — men, women, children, babies — living inside world cultures that are starving, war-torn, homeless, worse. All of it presented to me on television-shaped screens. First on home TVs. Much later from screens that I operate. That I can move through and around. That I can witness horrors I could never have known — fortunately, yes? — within the bland context of my own small life. Looking back I see how small my life has been. How small.

How can anything be worse? But yet *everything* is. Worse. And here I sit. Grumbling about my fairly mundane upper middle mundanities, little dilemmas, vexing small conundrums, the tits and tats of a class of American life that is perched, safely, here at the lower rung of a higher than average net worth. Living in a safe distant diaspora. What the heck?

What the hell do I think I can contribute to all those billions of printed words that I so casually stroll by at Barnes and Noble? I mean really. It's ludicrous. It's selfish. It's so, well, dumb. A waste of time, given, well, how many more years of it left for me? It is as if I have blinders on and cannot view the monumentally worse conditions of most other human lives on this same Earth that I lounge in. What is the point? I ask myself this question every day as I sit down in front of my computer considering another chapter for this work. Trying to tease out how on Earth we speak.

What is the point?

It's so hubristic. So self-involved. So blind. If anything is harder than self-censorship it feels like this is my personal bete noire. And the fact of my writing non-fiction autobiographical stuff, small stuff, well, isn't that presumptuous of me?

So isn't my being tongue-tied yet another example of the Binding of Women's Tongues? That I devalue my own culture and upbringing? Denigrating any possible value of what I may have to say to or within our current culture? Unless one is a woman 'influencer', with millions of followers online, who cares about one lone middle class woman approaching eighty doing a life review of a rather boring lifetime in a pleasant corner of a horrendous world? Ya gotta have some drama to put your story out there, Mary. Something salacious works well. Something shocking and gritty. Dirty. Creepy. Put some drama into your story, girl. But what if you have none? Then your tongue is as bound as was Sarah's in our very own scripture. You see? This is the thing. What's the point?

What is the point, Mary Carter?

What are you going to do now, Mary Carter?

A Proto-Influencer: Chicken Lady is Hatched

I did not do this to become an 'influencer'. I did not have any particular or defined or sub-rosa financial motivation behind my starting to write about my chickens on the infant, and at that time, the very tiny internet. The internetini, so to speak. Nobody in that sphere, using digital means to communicate with one another — nobody I do believe had an inkling of what they were starting when they started participating by 'talking' on The WELL.

How I and my chickens got to The WELL, not knowing a thing about internet — small 'i' at that time — or anything online or digital nor anything about computers outside of using a computer to compose copy for client advertising, I was somewhat magically drawn to a table at a local bookstore, piled high with books by Howard Rheingold: *The Virtual Community.* Published in 1993 its cover featured the words:

Homesteading on the Electronic Frontier.

Clueless, I grabbed a copy and virtually 'flew' home to see what it was all about. I rushed in to Gary shouting: "Gar. Gar. I don't know a thing about what's in this book. But I know it's something we absolutely need to know about."

And so we set out for places, for virtual LIVES, we had never known existed, but which we entered, strangers in a strange land. Sound familiar? And in my case, it would turn out to be me and my chickens.

It was stunning. Howard Rheingold presented this world of people communicating all the human experiences — life, illness, marriage, birth, elation, death, plus every human feeling I could imagine, and all of it accessible by way of computers. At that time the interface was Picospan, a digital method of keyboard hunt-and-peck, how prophetic that would be for this future Chicken Lady. When it came to developing the digital interface for this digital form of communication, the people who were pioneers on this new-spangled WELL invention made things up as they went along. They developed 'rules and regulations' — so to speak — for how this new entity would function and how we were to speak on The WELL. Early on, there were only a few hundred people working on this project. I cannot believe that, at that point in time, that any of them could have anticipated the impact and the eventual monumental numbers of people, worldwide, who would be connected by these means and who are, today, even more powerfully connected by these devices and techniques. And much of it started with Steward Brand and Howard Rheingold and many brilliant people would join and build this ineffable construct that began its place on the Internet — cap I — as The Whole Earth 'Lectronic Link — The WELL.

Two things in particular stood out for me as 'rules' I could not only abide by, but increasingly, that I would find lacking in today's online communities, here and now in 2025.

One: YOYO Words — You Own Your Own Words. And that means that whatever you write in your online messaging, you own. It is, in effect, the assurance that you own your own words and that they are copyrighted. For your use only. And they may be used with permission by someone else and only with your permission.

Two: The WELL wants to know, and record, your real name

when you join. There may be nicknames that you can adopt, but when you sign on as a member, it is NOT anonymous. This may seem archaic in light of today's internet filled to overloaded with godknowswho saying godknowswhat at any godknowstime. It's a free for all now and it's not pretty out there/here.

Two simple pledges we made to and on The WELL, but all the difference in the world for human, humane, conversation, — for empathy, ethics, courtesy — NOT being anonymous makes all the difference in the world to online communities and how they talk.

But I harp.

So, after speed-reading, aloud, Howard Rheingold's *The Virtual Community*, Gary and I signed up on The WELL. After a self-guided tour of topics and voices, I entered the Miscellaneous Domain with:

"I have a flock of chickens. Would anybody like to hear about them?"

Within a few moments — the length of time for several WELL members to peck out a response to my query, my life changed.

What might the development of The WELL have to do with the Akedah?

Of course I was not to make a connection for many years between my stint as the proto-blogger, the Chicken Lady, and my life as a student of *Torah*. But from my perspective now, with a dozen years since my own mikvah and a dozen years immersed in *Torah* study I begin to gather threads of similarity and dis-similarity between The WELL and the Akedah. What stands out immediately is that every member of the early WELL has a voice and may use their individual voice to communicate with and to hear other voices, regardless of station in life, male or female, class or stature, or any other ways that human beings define themselves when they speak to one another. Owning your own words is fundamentally important during WELL 'talk'. And I believe significantly, good clear communication also depends upon taking personal responsibility for what you say. Thus, having your identity known — with no anonymous souls with you online, can make a world of difference and of clarity in spoken communication. Now, sadly, there are millions of anonymous 'talkers' on today's internet and thus it is rife with mean and or evil words and misinformation and disinformation — you name it, but it's not good. Also there are gaps and omissions and missing words from millions of people who do NOT answer all those other spoken words. The small number of WELL members back in 1994, with their names well known, and during that early era, there were few who were merely seeking to be nothing but babbling 'influencers' — so that The WELL was more personal, kinder even, during disputation, it was simply, a better place to speak and to be heard, than today's monster-website jungle, overwhelmed with all rage, all the time?

When I ask: What might the development of The WELL have to do with the Akedah? I believe that at least a portion of it is that, on The WELL we were not anonymous. Same with *Torah* students — generally we are not anonymous. We reside in small classes. We appear in print with midrashim under our own names. Yet, if there are silences in our readings or missing elements, it is very likely that a student or a professor or another Jewish voice will step up to explore missing elements in our *Torahs*. And this kind of probing of scripture is accepted and assured in Jewish studies. One Jew. Five opinions. Same as when The WELL was new where I first learned about how on Earth to speak on the Internet.

Remember Her?

Excerpt of Sample post from 1995 on The WELL by The Chicken Lady.

Pecking Away. That's me!

Carmina is molting. And Daphne. Actually, Carmina had started to molt about a year ago and had haphazardly lost feathers from her neck. But her metabolism, weakened, I suppose, from producing so many hen-buster eggs, had seemed incapable of replacing the feathers, so she spent the past year scraggly-necked. Still proud, but scroungy looking, she stood listlessly in the hen house. The whole process picked up, however, with the shorter Fall days. She started to lose feathers from all over her once massive body. They drifted off in the straw leaving patchy bald areas, not unlike a man with male pattern baldness gone awry.

As the months of her molt dragged on, she started to weaken and to lose weight. I would reach up to touch her during her vulnerable somnambulism after dusk and feel her breastbone riding along her perch. I would feel the distinctive keel of it pressing against the loose chicken flesh of her thinning feather covering. She, proud and suspicious, would rise up on her legs on the perch, and revert to petulant peeping. Sometimes my fingernail would catch on a tuft of her dry, thin feathers and pull a little clump of them away as I pulled my hands back from her bony frame.

Then, as if on cue, as if nature insisted that all the hens work in flocking unison, Daphne lost all of her feathers. Actually, this was not precipitate, but happened over a period of about ten days. I would find a billowing mass of Daphne's feathers floating across the straw in the light evening breeze. And Daphne would stand there with feathers sticking out at odd angles all over her body. And then, it seemed, I went in one morning to feed everybody and there Daphne stood on the straw, naked. As good as. She had lost all the feathers on her entire belly, under her wings and on her neck. And all her tail feathers, that distinctive hands at prayer array of 'fingers at prayer' feathers, all of these were gone, leaving a soft round fleshy pink rump. As she perched, I could look up at her pink round butt and stomach and I shivered for her. She was peevish and would utter small hoarse throat sounds when

I patted her. No longer fat and robust, Daphne now looked dour. She, too, had gotten quite thin, with no bulging chicken drumsticks or breast, and a shriveled crop.

By now the days were getting shorter and dusk worked its way up the hillside starting around three in the afternoon. Luckily the nights were uncharacteristically warm. But, still, I worried that the two molting hens would get chilled. So I brought them inside.

Well, this all took place during the days before my big birthday weekend. You know, BIG. As in 50 years old. To mark the occasion I put on a big birthday party and casually invited all my friends, old and new. What I hadn't counted on was everybody accepting. Well, almost. The party drew friends to me from LA, Sacramento, and the whole Bay Area. I was so touched that so many of my friends made the effort to come. Really surprised and touched. The two most special friends who made it were the two I would have said would not have come. In fact one of them, Carol Kindle, declined immediately, citing a work conflict. This didn't hurt my feelings because I know she and her husband have their own business and frequently cannot make it to parties. My other friend, Matti Maloney, has not been able to get up to visit me at our new home since we moved here, ten years ago. But Matti called me immediately after receiving the invitation and said she wouldn't miss it for anything. Then, shortly before the party weekend, Carol Kindle e-mailed and said plans had changed and she'd be there, too. So.

Matti Maloney and Carol Kindle are friends from my other life. We were all in advertising together in the seventies and early eighties. Carol Kindle was the first person to hire me as an advertising copywriter and Matti hired me several years later along in my advertising career. In one of those moves you make to further experience, you find exceptional human warmth and lifelong comradeship. But not without a lot of struggle first. The advertising business puts constraints upon friendship, replacing your natural urges to share and nurture with urges to beat out your competition. To fight, to challenge, to thump your chest at your adversaries. For women, this means dropping the maternal, the soft, and taking on, instead, authoritarianism. Carol Kindle used to scare the living daylights out of me every time she read my copy. Her criticisms were disciplinarian and I had to write things over and over under her tutelage. But, you know what? She was right. I was a crummy writer. Promising. But crummy. Self indulgent. Blithering. Long winded.

'Start here' she would poke the center of the page, 'not up there at the beginning.' And she was right. All I had been doing for the first paragraph was metaphorical throat-clearing.

Now Matti Maloney was a different story. She got the benefit of Carol Kindle's rigorous training, plus a couple of other creative directors I had worked with by the time Matti hired me. So I was a half way decent advertising writer by then. But what we faced was our own faces in the ladies room mirror, getting older, getting harder, turning into 'those women'. We drank and complained. Drank and whined. Drank and raged. Sitting hunched in the euphemistic downstairs conference room, a dark and rodent-infested cocktail lounge, we would order yet another round with just a graceful flick of forefinger to the rim of the glass. If we were competitors, we had long since relaxed that role because now we were friends.

We were all so young and beautiful then. Young and pockets full of money. Young and still impressed by our own accomplishments in this 'sophisticated' advertising career. We loved advertising, Matti Maloney and Carol Kindle and I.

Then a lot of intervening stuff happened. The usual. Mid-life crises. All three of us came down with them, right on schedule. Which is not to denigrate their impact, but simply to telegraph them here. Dream-tormented, I went off to paint and left my advertising persona to rot somewhere in my synapses. Carol Kindle had children. Matti Maloney quit, equivocated, then had a baby. We all stopped drinking. Maybe not totally, but noticeably. And we drew apart. The phone call years I call them.

At first I was so sulky and indulgent in my studio, I barely communicated at all with Matti and Carol. Eating up my solitude and making up for lost time, I painted in a compulsion of creativity. Finally, gradually, and sporadically, I would join either Carol or Matti for lunch. Distracted visits, me feeling like I really needed to get back to my singular ridiculous obsession. But we listened to each other. We heard each other. We spoke the same language, still. And we narrated the stories of our lives, made tableaus for one another to illustrate what was happening back at our homes, back with our husbands, back there somewhere. What do women talk about? What animates female lunchtime conversations? What is said? What does it mean?

The weekend of my birthday, Matti Maloney and Carol Kindle came to be with me. I was edgy and nervous about the party. About the food. About the wine. Who would make it. Who would not.

Funnily enough, what Matti and Carol wanted most was to visit the hen house. I mean, not just courteous little noises to go out and see the chickens, but insisting on it. And it was just about the most important thing I could think of to have them do on this big birthday weekend. So we babbled a bit and hugged and kissed and edged our way out the back door, talking about our dreams, our work, our lives, and scuffled along the Fall pathway to the Chateau Le Coop.

I warned Carol and Matti to mind their shoes and the chicken poops as we lumbered in, party guests of a sort, a hen party I would quip, but for the unfortunate connotations.

Then Matti sat down on the doorjamb between the old and new wings of the Chateau and Carol deftly found a clean space to sit on the new bale of straw and I sat on my knees and we just talked. One by one, the hens and rooster would swirl and circle and come close enough for Carol or Matti to reach out and run a hand along their shining feathers as we chatted about this and that. The rooster was tall and big and shining and he made deep chesty sounds and looked at them intently with his big brown steady gaze. His floppy red comb dapper as a Frenchman's beret over one eye.

We sat in companionable silence. Knowing we could talk or not. Make sense or not. Could cry or make a dumb remark or laugh inappropriately. Could be together without constraint. We three friends, sitting among the hens. Almost fifty, each of us. Silent.

Then stirring. Our murmuring conversation lifting no further than the yellow straw and slightly muffled by its acoustics. I looked from Carol Kindle to Matti Maloney. Matti to Carol. And we drifted, every so often one of us reaching out to pat a passing hen, to glide our palms along a feathery back all the way out to the pert hands-at-prayer tail feathers. Three women. Friends. And, even as we sat there, I knew that time was slowing down so that I would be forced to notice this, to place a punctuation mark around our shoulders for emphasis, to hold us sitting here, forever, in my memory.

When my hens molt they receive their instructions through a bit of DNA. It schedules them to shed, then to replace, their feathers. One by one, old, worn feathers drop by the wayside. One by one, stout new feather shafts poke up through the hen's bare, pink skin. The shafts, receiving further messages from silent genes, aggressively, inexorably, produce, first fringe, then fluffy new feathers. Normally this process moves swiftly so the hen is only moderately inconvenienced by her ridiculous nakedness. And, swiftly, she is completely rehabilitated and she stands on the straw, blooming in her female pulchritude, a new hen.

The message, emitting from one of the thousands of beads of a hen's DNA molecule, is to change. To change from head to toe. And whether the hen can read the message, or not, can hear it or feel it or rationalize it, or not, does not matter. Because she will change without any of these.

I suppose it's logical to project that such a molecule exists in human females, too. That there is hidden somewhere on the chain of DNA an instruction which urges change. It doesn't take much observation to see that we change. Three friends of twenty years can see changes on the surface of the faces across the table.

Carol Kindle, Matti Maloney, and me, Chicken Lady.

Oh, sure, and hairdos, waistlines, the hunch of shoulder in a blouse. But these are but the surface residues of more fundamental, more elemental, biological changes within her soul. We shed whole personas, entire constructs of thought and feeling. Who'd a thunk? Who'd a thunk the competitive women who energetically produced words

for a clown-whale, words for selling turkeys, words for hawking fast food and low finance--who would have thought that they'd sit in delicate silence together with the hens? That they could shed so thoroughly, all the way down to nakedness, entire personalities? Entire cultures? Values? Dreams and aspirations? And that some time later, on a special birthday, we three friends would sit companionably in my hen house, beautiful and new, like all the other transformed females in our midst.

October 2025

Ah. So.
Here we are.
Still.
Not so bad.
Eighty,
Finally.

Out of the cosmos, resembling a post from NASA, like a Hubble image taken from zillions of light years away from Earth, from among billions of starlike objects, from nothing but air and clouds and comets and from a mother's heart's desire came a baby. Me. And who'd a thunk — me and the atomic bomb on a computer, no less, right here together today August 5, 2025. Siblings? Twins?

For all you dinner companions who asked me:

"So. Do you write about your own life in your novels?"

I say:

“Yeah. So what’s it to ya?”

You think that’s easy? You think that act diminishes my gifts as a writer of fiction? Easy? Writing from ‘your own life’ is not very creative, you may think to yourself, slurping yer soup. Oops, splashes onto yer shirt, buddy. Spaz. Probably not interesting ya think. Certainly, not difficult, that kind of writing? Well then, gloat. With yer preconceived notions. Slurp yer soup and feel all superior. Women write about luv. Little ‘l’. Men write about the World — big ‘W’ — history, wars, monarchies. Worse still is yet another dinner companion who says to me:

“Oh, I never read fiction. Only non-fiction.”

Ya mean like history, wars, monarchies?

What follows now is an excerpt from a chapter in my 2024 award-winning, novel *Diaspora of the Discombobulated,*

WINNER 2024 New Mexico-Arizona Book Awards. Out of the mouth of a Guardian Angel, a character I created out of whole cloth, if you please. Wings and all. Here is an excerpt from something my fictional Guardian Angel said in that book:

An Excerpt from the words of my fictional character Hannah-Naomi:

> *Words and words and words — intoned in haste, bitter words, spat out or hissed between clenched teeth — so many brands of hurtful words can cause pain. And, oh yes, they can and do: Kill.*
>
> *Once a year, at multiple times during the High Holy Days on the Jewish Calendar, members of Synagogues, all over the world, repeat the admonishments of the Al Chet. This recitation contains forty-four statements. All members of each congregation stand and repeat aloud and make amends for all forty-four mistakes, or transgressions, or sins — whichever Torah translation you may have. The reading proceeds aloud and, between each point, each and every member of the congregation takes responsibility for making amends and gently taps the heart in repentance:*
>
> *Tap. Tap.*
>
> *It does not matter if a single person in the room*

can say:

"Well, I never did that one. So, I'm clean of that mistake. Whew!"

But that's not how the Al Chet recital works. Standing and repeating in unison, and aloud, all forty-four mistakes, means that every single Jewish person takes responsibility for each and every single mistake listed in the Al Chet.

The scholars, the rabbis, knew the power of words for destruction and the creation of actual physical harm.

The Al Chet is long on specifics addressing the mistakes that can cause harm. It is, however, somewhat of a mystery as to its origins. It may date back to an era during the first diaspora of Secular Jews. Perhaps dating to the destruction of the Second Temple. Perhaps before even that time. When some communities of Jews moved away from the center of the Jewish World, they tried to maintain ritual and observance. And, without the handy instant communication of our present era — if not annoying, those digital modes of information retrieval — citizens in far-away diasporas would write down their questions to the scholars and wise commentators in distant Jerusalem. It must have taken months or years to get responses. The answers to their questions were referred to as Responsa. These written responses to the questions are recorded in vast volumes — in numerous books and in documents. Responsa have continued throughout Jewish history and may continue right up to the present day in the 21st Century. Some of the Responsa were closely held as secret and were communicated by spoken word only. Some were simple enough to be addressed in a single one page letter.

Within the Al Chet, out of the forty-four statements, fully nine use the word speech or imply the way mouths and speech are presented as mistakes. Words such as "endless babbling" or "insincere confession" or "foolish speech" or "vulgar speech" and "scornful scoffing". Taken as a whole, of course, the entire Al Chet implies the use of words and language within each of the definitions of all forty-four statements.

Remember this about the Al Chet: the congregation, as a whole, stands, and repeats the entire Al Chet aloud, together. The congregation, as a whole, takes responsibility, repeating the words of all forty-four Al Chet statements with a gentle Tap, Tap, to each and every heart in the congregation as it pays heed to its own responsibility to make next year a better year.

"Yes, Tap, Tap, I take upon my conscience the actions defined very skillfully in the words I am repeating in this moment's recitation of the Al Chet. And, even if I, this

member of this congregation, have never committed a particular mistake on this very long list, even though innocent, yes, I take heartfelt responsibility for recognizing this form of spoken mistake"

Tap. Tap.

And people still maintain that the spoken word doing damage, causing pain, and chaos, and you still dare to say out loud and to make your excuse to me that:

"Well it's just words. Words can't kill you."

That glib admonishment is not true.

The scholars, rabbis, and wise authors of the Al Chet specifically mention the word speech, drawing particular attention to the harms that can be done by mere speech.

And you still persist in saying:

"Well, mere words cannot kill you."

Well, yes, I must contradict:

In fact: they can. They do.

Kill.

I do not mean to harp. I do not speak here by way of sermonizing. But, Chava, you might do well to remember, Angels are prone to harping. We are always in a flap about something.

So listen now to me:

Words, hasty and hot, can kill desire, can kill enthusiasm, can kill inspiration, aspiration, creation. Words, so-

called mere words, can kill souls and deprive them of the energy needed for a soul's evolution into fulfillment. And a soul is not unlike an Angel — nobody has ever seen one. Yet a soul can be killed. And whether remembered or evoked at a later date by a Guardian Angel who uses memory as a teaching tool, in whatever form and especially spoken loud enough to do their damage, words can kill and have done. I knew this and I saw the power of spoken words to leave indelible damage on the lives of two artists to whom I was tasked with Guardian Angel work. A man and a woman, once children, carrying the wounds of words and words and words. The swift cuts of gossip, so-called, mere. Remarks hissed, barely audible, through clenched teeth, snide rejoinders, over and over and over again. . . .

Just words, nevermind. Can't kill you. Right?

Words, spoken with a barely audible breath or precisely articulated, shouted even, words will make their mark. Words can hit the unguarded target of a person's heart. And the heart, with its own reasons, may absorb a lifetime's barrage of words as surely as suffering multiple punches to the gut. And those words will pulse and bypass spleen and gall bladder, flying straight into the nearby loyal, ever-beating heart. Eventually such a heart, repeatedly exposed to killing words, the heart, finally, stuttering, can barely function. The heart will however maintain its scars and always has reasons of its own that reason knows nothing of. It may be rational to say:

"Well, it's just words. Words cannot kill you."

But no. The heart retains cruel words, and beats despite pain and injury, beats erratically, barely audible, despite its lifetime burden of words. Words may injure and will endure, for a lifetime — the single lifetime of a single human being — causing injury that may last for decades, leaving the injured human adrift, half dead or, indeed, completely numb, barely conscious, blinded in a dark and numb fugue.

Words have killed. Have killed all kinds of aspiration. Killed dreams. Killed creativity.

Dedication Too

It was not a requirement of my new Jewish self, after my mikvah, that I re-marry my husband of nearly fifty years. Yet, Gary and I had a re-dedication of our marriage vows when we were in our seventies. Our ceremony together was to commemorate and to seal my major life change. Our words, an assurance to the cosmos of our destinies that we are committed to our new life together.

I'm a little slow at times. Slow on the uptake. Slow on the interpretation of words spoken by me and to me — words of a friend. It has taken me eight decades to notice this significant factor in one of my most longtime friends.

We're both in our eighties now. And I simply did not notice that she is the only 'girlfriend' of mine whose mother died when my friend was just about to graduate from high school. An untimely death. And I had also lost my mother to an untimely death. My mother was diagnosed as terminal just weeks after I had graduated from college. We both had weathered these events — I had been a bit older but by no means a fully functioning grown-up when this all happened. My friend had been surrounded by brothers and sisters and was bound in her own heart to take care of them all after their mother's death. I, of course, was a singleton, bound in my own soul to survive, somehow, somewhere, some time. Two of us. We gradually became friends and confidants over several decades. She a reticent speaker. Me, jokey and self protective and glib, always withholding. The first time she told me about her mother's untimely departure, all I can recall is a sort of sinking realization that went like this in the back of my mind:

"Ah, yes. She too."

I could not yet elaborate on my own similarity to her experience with loss. I had been, now as I look back I see — I had been too tightly bound in the self-imposed reticence, and darkness, of my silent fugue. A self-protective garb I drew around me protecting or secreting my history by not telling anybody about my experiences of my loss. I pulled around myself a guarded choice of words as I learned, early on after my mother's funeral, that potential friends of mine back then would draw away if I spoke the words death, dying, dead. So I learned to not say those words. Thus to wedge myself even more snuggly and tighter into my benighted space. She, my new friend back then, both in our twenties when we first met, was just a measure more able to speak about her losses and her mother's death. She, a twin, with her sister as her companion forever in their mortality. She, my friend, never seemed to be alone in the existential sense of being lone in the cosmos. So I was able to hear, from them both, the twins, in the juxtapositions of twin-language, an exchange they could do in conversation where each of them filled in for the other as they went through the narrative of their lives after the death of their mother. And I listened. And I learned, gradually, how to tell their respective tones of voice and their individuations of personality by their voices and their patterns of speaking. And, as the decades progressed between our sporadic visits, I could even recognize their telephone voices.

So how come I missed the foundational bedrock of our friendship as it evolved into middle age, then into what is named old-age and then into actually becoming too-old ladies?

That she and I, this twin, this person surrounded by siblings who needed her more than anyone after they all had lost their mother — how had she been able to speak so clearly about how the death of her mother affected them all? She and I were so different within our losses. Yet, lasting into this ripe decade and suddenly I realize — she is the only woman friend of mine to this very day whose mother died out of time and place and the only woman friend who can bear to hear the words death, dying, and dead without drawing away, wincing. But, instead, she can hear my words with full attention and sensitive discernment. She is my one friend with whom I may speak candidly about unimaginable losses and the effects of unspeakable pain from my past. And she listens with intention. And she allows me to refer to that final hospital visit, for example, without guiding me away from this unbearable topic. And she can listen, for example, to my experience of one of my cats dying recently and she can understand how much more intense and gut-wrenching were my sobs over the loss of that precious kitty than even over the loss of my own mother, way, very much too far, way back then. And as I spoke to her about the loss of my kitty, I felt a shadow of guilt hovering over my words. I was anxious that she might not like what I had just admitted to. I felt guilty for admitting to this kind of intensity of grieving over a cat. But she got it. On her own most attentive levels of consciousness. This friend got it. She understood and could identify with this kind of display of a very separate variety of loss. A mother dies. A cat dies. And she, my friend, does not back away from my pain, but acknowledges it as familiar. And she did not scoff at it. Nor did she reprimand me for my shallowness. For being too sensitive. And I knew it. And I somehow had pieced together our mutual experiences of grieving. And she knew what I had meant by that kind of deep grief. A mother dies. A beloved cat dies. How hard it is to go through both kinds of loss, the latter a reincarnation of the former. And with her chosen words, she helps me to not feel guilty about a certain variety of grieving compared to another unimaginable kind of grieving. She got it. She did not turn away from the topic. She did not scold me for callousness nor for being over-sensitive. She was familiar with the same losses herself, including, of course, that rough foundational one of the death of a mother too soon in life.

So it takes me eight decades to realize she is the only woman friend of mine who has for me this kind of connection, to one another, and about what had been gained, for both of us, in experiencing our losses of the untimely deaths of our mothers. About losses and gains we both received, throughout our remaining lives. There were many things gained, for each of us, through the deaths of our mothers. Which is a perverse kind of gain — isn't it? Our mothers died in untimely departures. What, exactly, had we gained?

Around the time of my awakening from my dark decade, I found solace in my friend's garden to begin to think and to remember my life. Couldn't have been more than in my mid-thirties. But at last I could begin to be present in those moments that I had for so long buried. My friend's gardens provided me with the same acceptance that she, herself, had done over the earliest years of our friendship. Non-judgmental. Listen mindfully to what had been buried for so many a sunrise, sunset.

My friend and her beloved husband attended our Jewish wedding — under the chuppah with words spoken and recorded in scripture by Ruth:

"Do not entreat me to leave you, to return from following you, for wherever you go, I will lodge: your people shall be my people and your God my God . . . Where you die, I will die and there I will be buried." Ruth

This book is dedicated to that friend. For Joann O.

I Am Born.

1945 October

"My Darling,

I arrived at the hospital about 1: 45 A.M. and the baby was born at 8:01 A.M. When I went, I thought sure it would take longer than that as labor hadn't even started at that time — but it came on suddenly about 3:00 (I think) and they took me into the delivery room about 5:15 and the doctor got there about 5:45. She had to rush down as they hadn't expected it to happen so soon. And from 6:20 (there was a clock in the room which I looked at every time I could) to about 7:30 I don't remember very much except I was under ether most of the time and naturally couldn't feel everything but enough so I knew what the doctor was telling me to do and also enough so I was glad someone had invented ether. Then from about 7:30 to about 8:02 it was more like a dream with sound effects and some sensation but I couldn't see as the mask was over my face. All through the whole thing I felt I wanted to hurry as much as I could — a couple of times I almost automatically asked the nurse how much longer it would be. It was a strange sensation

— I would vaguely think — then I would hear myself talking, as if it were someone else in another room. In fact, a rather funny thing happened — a woman in the next room had a little boy about half an hour before my baby came — I could hear her doctor or someone say it was a boy and I thought it was mine and I felt glad it was over — then I suddenly realized that it wasn't over. After that I kind of went out again I guess to sleep. I don't know — it was like a dream again — and the next thing I was aware of was a baby crying—just a little at first and the doctor saying "come on now, come on" then the mask was lifted up a little and I raised my head just a little and saw the baby lying on a table with a couple of nurses working over her. I really felt relieved then. I have more to write, but am feeling tired more. More for later!

I Love You,
XXXX from me
xxxx from baby

Within her numerous letters sent overseas, throughout her pregnancy, my mother had thought I would be a twin. Her doctor predicted it. There were twins in my mother's family. There are several war letters speaking of twins to be born — what to name them for example. Those letters and their assured references to twins really surprised me. The rest of her letters, after my birthday, love letters to and about me, were filled with her mother's extravagant love. That I was the most beautiful baby. That I had a sense of humor. How smart I was. Her intense mother's love would subsume her love for my father while they were separated by war. Not knowing if he would return, ever. He, The Pilot, always requiring that love be a zero-sum game, would never get over my place in her affections.

I have just one memory-image of my birthday — I am wrapped firmly in a bunting blanket and am being lifted and borne down a hallway with green tiles and I have an as yet inarticulate sense of dread.

I Had a Dream Last Night

I had a dream last night.

It was during the eve of my turning eighty. Birthday Eve, yes?

Now that I am in my 81th year I have dozens of dreams. Ephemeral. Scattered. Vanished by sunrise. Dreams and ordinary sleeplessness. I wake up from most of my dreams with no memory of them. Except this one that happened at mid-October of 2025. I recall it now quite clearly.

I had a dream last night.

I am returning to my first apartment after my college graduation. The building offers about a dozen one bedroom apartments. This building is Spanish style, overlooking a garden area with mature trees and shrubs. My apartment has a balcony, upon which I and my friends sit — so various the friends back then — and we watch the sun go down.

In this dream I walk into my apartment, into its postage stamp entryway, and turning left, I glance in habit to my left and up to where the ceiling meets the walls of the living room and note that the water stain up there is now gone. Perhaps mended in its leaking some years ago.

In my dream, my apartment is completely empty, very clean, walls bright and, as I note, unstained by leaks as it had been back then when I had moved in just a few days after college graduation. Commencing, I didn't have the smarts to use that word back then, commencing upon whatever would be my life. And at $95 a month, completely affordable on my Bullocks, first job ever as a salesgirl in the bra department. Oy. Well, it's certain I did not have Oy in that girls' vocabulary of mine.

So the dream last night was me walking around that apartment. Clean, empty, white walls, no leaks, and bright sunshine just like it had been back then. I walked around the living room, the dining area, and kitchen. In the kitchen I commented to somebody in my dream about the counter tops and how small and cramped they had been and how I created real fancy gourmet meals and there one such meal sat, posing dreamlike, displayed with self-conscious sprigs of green and yellow garnish upon the tiny countertop of polished jeweled stone.

I walked all around that empty white apartment and noted to myself that it was empty. Blank. Not a sign of who I had been back then — no artwork tacked on the far wall for example. That apartment, was my first home away from home in the Fall of 1967, a bit after my commencement.

"What are we going to do now, Mary Carter?"

When I woke up from this pastiche of images from my earliest apartment, I was puzzled. How blank I felt, even though life now in this present tense is, for me, complicated with unbearable television-shaped images of someone's distant loved ones returning home after kidnapping and bondage and torture that had lasted, for them, two years. As I am now, burdened in my present moments of witnessing unbearable embraces, kisses, sobs as those distant strangers are reunited, my time in this present tense is filled with fear and anxiety and other peoples' pain. But what I felt upon awakening from my dream, waking up from that white and empty first apartment, with its image of a lavish meal I had created and placed lovingly upon my tiny kitchen counter, I felt as empty as my dream had been. For a few minutes I felt exactly that blank, especially in juxtaposition with my conscious reality today, mid-October 2025.

What could my dream have signified?

Perhaps an admonishment? Reminding me how empty had been my life at age 22 back then in 1967. Empty yet sunlit. Blank and empty. Utterly. And, as I lay in bed under my present-day flannel sheets, I re-experienced how empty I had been back then. No, really. I experienced a few moments of that earlier 'me' and realized that, back then, I had been so very empty of content or character or judgement or of insight.

And then, wham. My world, that little unformed sunny self, living in that sunny first apartment, was about to enter upon real life. Life, real. And I hadn't even suspected it.

Empty I had been.

I had a dream last night.

Driving over to be with my mother one morning during her long illness, I was listening to KFWB noisy rock and roll when the station announcer cut into the music and reported, crisp and serious, that Martin Luther King had been assassinated. I am not sure that the announcer used that word — assassinated. But in the weeks and years that passed, that would be the word. That would be the act that brought down Martin Luther King, Jr. That would be the end for him, a man, but never, not ever, for him would there be a synonym for assassination. That day, hearing that news, I pulled my car over to the curb, left the engine running, and sat there with my head against the steering wheel and I said aloud:

"I can't think about this right now. I have to go over to be with my mother. I cannot think about this right now."

That sad news buried in 1968 was not in the dream I had last night.

Unlike my dream last night, the person who was me back then, was in complete and utter darkness. The me of that dream was clear and sunlit, as yet unrevealed for who I would become. Instead, for a decade, I would dwell in utter blackness.

I am not certain when or by what means I heard Robert Kennedy say to a crowd in Indianapolis on April 4, 1968, these words:

Even in our sleep, pain which cannot forget falls
drop by drop upon the heart, until, in our own despair, against
our will, comes wisdom through the awful grace of God.

Robert F. Kennedy quoting ***Aeschylus*** *as he announced the assassination of Martin Luther King, Jr. at Indianapolis April 4, 1968*

Author's Afterword

How on Earth do we speak?

Why on Earth do I repeat this question so many times?

Why over and over again? Why in conjunction with my memories?

I did not forget Marc's 1967 graduation ceremony question:

"What are we going to do now, Mary Carter?"

I carried his question with me – repeating it at various junctures of my life. I would puzzle, at times, over its meaning. Yet I brought it ever into the present tense of my life and of how on Earth we speak, talk, communicate. Marc's question was with me at commencement and is with me still. So instead of just forgetting it upon its leaving Marc's tongue, I have cherished it. Brought it out of it's benighted probability of being lost in darkness back then, I have called Marc back into life. Maybe not ideal. Maybe not heroic, but possible. Entirely possible. Could have happened. Could have become my lover. Could have opened the cockpit doors. With love, Marc, from me.

Maybe this is how memory works to manage how on Earth

we speak? I don't know. But there you are.

"Now, what are you going to do Mary Carter?"

This book started with a question about no speech. About the absence of speech, words, about blankness within our sacred document: our *Torah*. How could a whole line of questioning hinge on NO THING? How could I start with one question, drawn from NOTHING and find enough steam to look back into my own very long life thus far? All this yak yak yak about No Thing? Really, there's a perversity to my focus. I have created a very wordy Commentary around a *Torah* portion that has NO words. If you have read thus far then you are very brave, very energetic, very patient indeed. And I thank you. What a peculiar turn of mind I must have to focus so many words that come from so few, nigh, totally missing words, the very absence of words. And to comment so very much upon so very little.

Well perhaps it's evidenced even in my own scoffing moniker for this past year of my living. 8T. Even I have abandoned words in who and how and by what spoken word or words that I call myself in this book, at this time of my life. Sheesh! It's catching!

And yet, I am deemed to be a Commentator. That this thing here is Commentary upon Jewish scripture. I am surprised and honored and a bit embarrassed that a good friend and teacher gave this book the honorific 'Commentary', raised my modest self-ascribed 'midrash' naming what I have written as Commentary — Cap. C.

It all comes back to the messages in the *Akedah* I suppose. Or not. Take your pick. Spoken messages. Missing messages. Implied messages. The implications of missing messages. And then Sarah died. But not a word from her after what must have been harrowing messages revealed to her after Abraham and Isaac returned home.

Women's voices, missing or removed, have been officially silent for too many eons. That's what the *Akedah* shows us when we study *Torah*, yet again here in 2025. Nothing much has changed in the literal words of scripture as we view it again and again, throughout our studies.

Then again there is yet another aspect to how on Earth we speak. What about elements of self-censorship included in how on Earth we speak? What I discover, working on this series of life stories, a memoire so to **speak**, is how I shuffle through thousands of memories and then how I decide to include a narrative of one thing or another. Or how NOT to include this or that memory of this or that episode from my way too many decades. How? How does my own self-censorship work? Why this event and not that event? Why do I focus upon so very many weird or ugly or unhappy or creepy events? Why do I select this and omit that in my self-narrative, here now that you read these in print, what say you, dear reader? I do not have a Redactor. I have no line editor for this volume. So how come I leave out so very many memories in the process of assembling my narrative – how come I leave out such an avalanche of recalled memories? If you think it is easy to sum up a lifetime of events and to then write from your own perspective, I ask you – how do you censor yourself? It may be glib to say, 'well, I will tell it all', but how on Earth does this thing – memory – work? How does memory relate to memoire?

And, surprising, yet very important: How come certain memories in this, my written narrative, cause me such visceral fear? Why has this occurred so many times during my writing of this memoire? Fear. I have experienced real, visceral fear. I wake in the night and vow I will NEVER publish this book. Out of shaking night terrors, I wake up deeply afraid. Some nightmares, even. No. Never will I publish. I vow this in the night, deeply shaken. How does that work?

Then morning breaks and I am confident again that I am writing something of – granted it may be just my ego pressing me forward – I see the manuscript as of at least some narrow form of importance. How on Earth can I speak? How on Earth does anybody speak?

Shifting now back to *Torah:*

And why, may I further ask, do I return to *Torah* for perspective about How on Earth we Speak? What's with that? And how do I question and argue with and about the formation of a particular portion dedicated to our matriarch, Sarah? What's with that part of this process? How did I notice her lack of voice in either her own speech or in the narration of her part of the binding of Isaac inside this *Torah* portion here, in 2025?

May I comment upon that *Torah* portion? Make of it Commentary? Is that suitable to do with *Torah* study? Is this suitable for memoire? Here in 2025?

Yet with the Taliban's interpretation of the same passage of scripture — for example — that is honored within all three religions — Christianity, Islam, and Judaism — is quite different, shocking even to those of us who study *Torah* these days. The Taliban have apparently determined, and put to use in daily observant life, another version of the *Akedah* altogether. Their interpretation, within their version of Islam, is demonstrated in this quote:

". . . Afghanistan's Taliban offered its congratulations to the American people for ". . . **not handing leadership of their great country to a woman** . . ."

The Taliban prohibits girls education past the sixth grade and recently banned the sound of women's voices outside their homes.

I am dumbfounded. Truly. And perhaps truly, in real life I

am made dumb by hearing that interpretation of scripture about words of women's voices.

This is so sputteringly horrifying, ignorant, a violent assault on all us girls out here, I don't know what to say. Speechless. Well, they'd sure be glad of that wouldn't they? Fill in for yourself words of spitting rage. F-words galore.

". . . not handing leadership of their great country to a woman . . .."

They, those Taliban, would righteously and with keen joy, watch, if our country, so called, went down. They would celebrate, indeed. So why why why celebrate our NOT handing leadership to women? Isn't that the very thing they desired? This is the twisted intellect of that all-male oligarchy.

How stupid they are when seen in their naked ignorant minds.

As I pointed out earlier in this book, from my own well-thumbed *Encyclopaedia Judaica Vol. 2 A-Ang page 482:*

"The Akedah influenced both Christian and Islamic thought . . . **The Akedah to the moralists was a fertile text for the inculcation of religious and ethical values. . .**"

It's a rabble out there. What the *Akedah* teaches all three religions, when they turn to the same quote from scripture, is wide open to further study. In our *Torah* classes, the *Akedah* is open to argumentation with narrative. It is not considered bad or sinful or disrespectful to question texts during our study sessions.

But listen now as you talk with other too-old women during lunch, perhaps. It is indeed the unbinding of singular women's tongues, telling, but also, importantly, *listening to* the strands and content of each other's lives and thoughts. The whole megillah. From the mouths of women. But it's only these few women. God knows there are billions more with things to say whose tongues are still, and summarily, bound.

If your beloved comes home one day to tell you all about how he or she almost killed your most beloved child, SAY something, FLING something, SHOUT something. Don't just die and you're done. Act. Speak. Unbind your tongue.

So now you're done reading this book. And so you think I didn't say it good enough, after all that *Akedah* stuff? And I shouldn't have said 'not good enough'. I should have said instead, 'not well enough'. I did not go deep enough? Not scholarly enough? Not interesting enough? Not even CORRECT? And you may observe, you as the astute reader that you are, that the Author was too emotional at times. Too angry. Not objective enough. A serious author includes statistics, quotes from reliable authorities with their recent studies on this or that. A serious author is by natural circumstances, male. He does not divert serious and important narratives into mere personal animus. And, what about that kink in the whole concept of Speaking: that of self-censorship? Now there's yet another complexity to consider.

Oh? Izatso?

Maybe I screwed up. Didn't do this thing right?

Well then do something yourself.

Well then: you go do it.

Do it better.

Make it better.

Go.

Do it.

Make your own statement. Use your own words. Unbind your own tongue.

You go girl!

Mary E. Carter 2026 New Mexico USA

Glossary
Jewish Words and Terminology

Mikvah A ritual bath used for spiritual purification. It is used primarily in conversion rituals and after the period of sexual separation during a woman's menstrual cycles.

Torah In its narrowest sense, Torah the first five books of the Bible: Genesis, Exodus, Leviticus, Numbers and Deuteronomy, sometimes called the Pentateuch or the Five Books of Moses. In its broadest sense, Torah is the entire body of Jewish teachings.

High Holy Days The holidays of Rosh Hashanah, the Days of Awe, and Yom Kippur are commonly referred to as the High Holidays or the High Holy Days.

Midrash From a root meaning "to study," "to seek out" or "to investigate." Stories elaborating on incidents in the Bible, to derive a principle of Jewish law or provide a moral lesson.

Talmud The most significant collection of the Jewish oral tradition interpreting the Torah.

Maimonides Rabbi Moshe ben Maimon, one of the greatest medieval Jewish scholars and author of Rabbinic commentary. Commonly referred to by the acronym 'Rambam'.

Shul School. The Yiddish term for a Jewish house of worship. The term is used primarily by Orthodox Jews.

Al Chet Lit. for the sin. A confession of community sins recited repeatedly on Yom Kippur. See Yom Kippur Liturgy.

Yahrzeit Yiddish: lit. anniversary. The anniversary of the death of a close relative.

Yom Kippur Lit. Day of Atonement. A day set aside for fasting, depriving oneself of pleasures, and repenting from the sins of the previous year.

Lashon Harah Lit. the evil tongue. Sins against other people committed by speech, such as defamation, gossip, swearing falsely, and scoffing.

Huppah The wedding canopy, symbolic of the groom's home, under which the wedding ceremony is performed.

Bashert Yiddish: fate, destiny. A soul mate, an ideal, pre-destined spouse. Any good or fortuitous match, such as the perfect job or the perfect house.

Parsha A weekly Torah portion read in synagogue. To find this week's portion, check the Current Calendar.

Mitzvah Lit. commandment. Any of the 613 commandments that Jews are obligated to observe. It can also refer to any Jewish religious obligation, or more generally to any good deed.

Beit Din Lit. house of judgment. A rabbinical court made up of three rabbis who resolve business disputes under Jewish law and determine whether a prospective convert is ready for conversion.

Grok To understand or to 'get'.

To find more Jewish words visit *jewfaq.org/glossary.htm*

Glossary
Flight and Airplanes

PBY The Consolidated Model 28, more commonly known as the **PBY** Catalina (U.S. Navy designation), is an American flying boat and amphibious aircraft designed by Consolidated Aircraft in the 1930s and 1940s. In U.S. and British WWII service.

Lenticular Clouds A high-altitude cloud that is shaped like a lens.

Cowling The term "**cowl**" means "hood." Cowlings are essentially hood-like coverings for engines. Many airplanes feature cowlings. They'll typically have a single cowling for each of their respective engines.

Aileron Either of two movable flaps on the wings of an airplane that can be used to control the plane's rolling and banking movements.

Selected References

- *The Bible With Sources Revealed* Richard Elliott Friedman
- Encyclopaedia Judaica
- *Torah A Women's Commentary* Tamara Cohn Eskenazi and Andrea Weiss
- *The Hebrew Bible A Translation With Commentary* Robert Alter
- *The Torah A Modern Commentary* Rabbi W. Gunther Plaut
- *Ernest's New Watch* Gary W. Priester
- *The Koren Shalem Humash with Rashi and Onkelos* Rabbi Lord Jonathan Sacks
- *The Way of the Boundary Crosser An Introduction to Jewish Flexidoxy* Gershon Winkler
- *Silences* Tillie Olsen
- *A Room of One's Own* Virginia Woolf

Acknowledgements

My grateful recognition goes to my four brave souls who were kind, patient, persevering, and thorough in their respective first reads of this book. All of them had busy lives and they took the time to pay attention to those early, very rough, manuscripts of mine.

All of my previous books and this one as well, were designed and put to type by my husband, Gary W. Priester.

He was an advertising art director for more than four decades, working on the accounts of corporate clients who could not have been as picky and demanding as I have been. He deserves an award for bravery for seeing my projects through from digital files to final pages. Oh, and I love him too — still.

Mary E. Carter 2026

Sarah Steinway, aged seventy-five, survives a catastrophic flood by moving into her treehouse on the northern shoreline of the San Francisco Bay. With snark and pluck, she lives up there for five years. Turning to Torah for comfort, she instead engages in argumentation with God, shouting the eternal question: "Why me?"

". . . by turns very funny and very serious, confident and uncompromisingly weird. Mary E. Carter has a voice with unquestionable power, and we look forward to reading more from her."

—Jewish Book Council

Available through Ingram and amazon

Whatever happened to Sarah Steinway? Find out in this sequel, All Good Tova Goodman Revised Edition. Readers will be surprised by the haunting conclusion of Mary E. Carter's Award-Winning Debut Novel, I, Sarah Steinway.

"Carter's page-turning portrait of a woman surviving the apocalypse is hauntingly memorable."

— Publishers Weekly

Available through Ingram and amazon

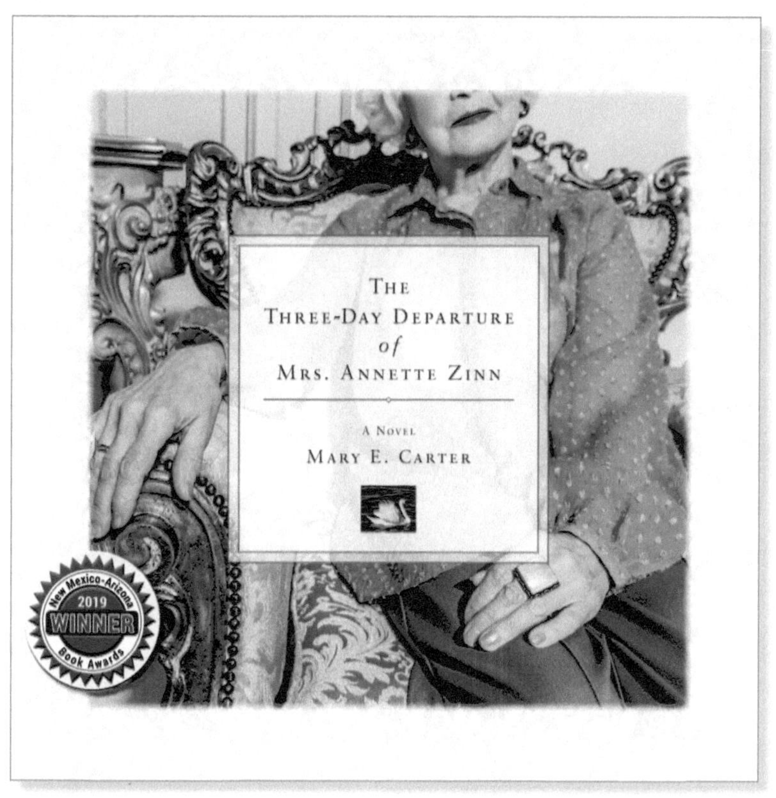

"I always look forward to getting to know Mary E. Carter's characters. The Jews, and the righteous non-Jews as well, have a pintele yid: a spark of Jewishness that helps them navigate this complex world with sensitivity. I enjoyed the exploration of the soul hovering for three days and was intrigued with the idea that it might remember details of events that were forgotten or hidden during its time in this world. During her three-day departure, Mrs. Annette Zinn discovers that her memories have the potential to serve as a blessing."

— Rabbi Jack Shlachter
Judaism for Your Nuclear Family, phisicsrabbi@gmail.com

www.ingramcontent.com/pod-product-compliance
Lightning Source LLC
LaVergne TN
LVHW090551110826
845146LV00001B/97